A TRUE AND COMPLE __

OF THE LIFE OF

WILLIAM ADAMS

-THE ENGLISH SAMURAI-

Act Two: Voyage to Japan

1598-1600

By Richard Irving

A TRUE AND COMPLETE ACCOUNT OF THE LIFE OF WILLIAM ADAMS -THE ENGLISH SAMURAI-

Act Two: The Voyage to Japan – 1598-1600

©Richard T. A. Irving 2021

All rights reserved by the author and the publisher. No part of this book may be reproduced or transmitted in any form or by any means graphic, electronic, or mechanical, including photocopying, recording, taping, or by any information storage retrieval system, without written permission from the publisher.

ISBN: 9798475743744
Imprint: Independently published

TABLE OF CONTENTS

PREFACE vi

ACKNOWLEDGEMENTS ix

I.   "So, in the yeare of our Lord God, 1598, I was hired for chiefe Pilot of a Fleete of five sayle, whiche was made readie by the chiefe of the Indian Company Peter Vanderbag, and Hance Vanderneke; the Generall of this Fleet was a Marchatt called Jaques Mayhay, in which ship, being Admirall, I was Pilot." 1

II.   "Loving Wife, you shall understand how all things have passed with me from the time of mine absence from you. We set saile with five ships from the Texel in Holland the four and twentieth of June, 1598. And departed the Coast of England the fift of July." 16

III.   "...the Pilots should be no more in the Councell..." 22

IV.   "...and many of our men were sick..." 35

V.   "... Raine, Winde, Snow, Hayle, Hunger, losses of Anchors, spoyles of Ship and Tackling, Sicknesse, Death, Savages; want of store, and store of wants, conspired a fulnesse of miseries." 48

VI.   "...but in long travels we lost our whole Fleet." 61

VII.   "So against their wils they made composition with us, which within the time appointed they did accomplish." 79

VIII.   "... it was resolved to go for Japon" 90

IX.   "...the people did us no harme, we not understanding each other, but by signes and tokens." 111

X.   "Comming before the King, he viewed me well, and seemed to be wonderfull favourable." 125

XI.   "...all we that were left alive, came together again." 137

APPENDIX ··· 146
NOTES AND SOURCES ·· 155
ENDNOTES ·· 160

PREFACE

William Adams is generally recognized as 'the first Englishman in Japan'. More than that, he became a favourite of the Japanese Shogun – Tokugawa Ieyasu – and was made a samurai. He was given *hatamoto* status, denoting his position as personal retainer to the most powerful lord in the land and close advisor on all matters relating to foreign affairs. From a British perspective he is officially remembered for having assisted in negotiating the first ever British trade treaty with Japan. More popularly, he is remembered as THE ENGLISH SAMURAI. This is his story.

The full story of William Adams is an epic of adventure and deserves more than just a brief history of his life encapsulated in a single volume. In this project, the drama that was his life is retold in five Acts. Act One recounts William's early years - from his birth in the town of Gillingham in 1564; the same year that William Shakespeare entered this world. It tells of how his father, John, a shipwright, had moved there following the expansion of the Queen's naval facilities on the River Medway. For twelve years, and from the age of twelve, William was apprenticed to a young mariner named Nicholas Diggens, with whom he formed a bond akin to brotherhood. At the age of 24 Adams became a master mariner himself and took command of a small armed merchant ship called the *Richard Duffield*; and he set sail to fight the Spanish armada.

Originally assigned to carry supplies from London to the main fleet at Plymouth, the *Richard Duffield* was soon engaged as a fighting vessel throughout the campaign. After this, Adams' ship carried goods for the Barbary trade, carrying sugar from Morocco, as well as the raw materials upon which the newly emerging publishing industry in London was dependent. Trade was rarely carried on peacefully, however, and William had to be prepared always for fights at sea with Spanish galleys, Barbary corsairs, and other pirates. It is even likely he carried a 'letter of reprisal' himself, giving him status as a privateer.

At the age of 33 years, William was told of an expedition which planned to head for the east – the very far east – to profit from trade in spices. He was invited to join a Dutch ship departing Rotterdam as pilot, or navigator, to help guide them to the exotic islands of Ternate, Tidore, and Ambon, and also to Japan. It was indeed an opportunity to make 'little experience of the small knowledge which God had given him'. Act One ends with William Adams, his brother Thomas, and a small band of other English mariners setting sail to Rotterdam to join the Dutch expedition. Here, Act Two continues the story of their fateful (and, for many of them, fatal) voyage to Japan.

In short, Act Two tells of a disastrous voyage, but one which is filled with tales of adventure and discovery. It tells of how five Dutch ships sailed from Rotterdam; of how William became ill with fever and nearly died; of how the fleet became trapped in the Magellan Strait and had to survive the harsh winter months there; of how so many were killed by spears and arrows when trying to find food and water on the coast of Chile; of how the surviving crews deceived the Spanish colonial authorities and escaped into uncharted waters of the Pacific Ocean; it tells of further storms and the loss of ships; and it tells of false charts, making it an almost impossible task to find Japan. Finally, it tells of how Adams and just twenty-four other survivors on the *Liefde*, the sole remaining ship, made it to Japan; and of how Williams Adams was separated from the others and interrogated – by Tokugawa Ieyasu himself.

ACKNOWLEDGEMENTS

Robin Maynard, Derek Massarella, and Timon Screech each gave up their time to read through the first, rather rough, draft of this manuscript and then spent a great deal more of their time making extremely useful and constructive comments. Thank you, all of you, for the encouragement you gave me to carry on and complete this project. Any errors of fact or interpretation are entirely mine, but those few instances where fact and fiction may blur will, I hope, continue to provide an excuse for hearty dialogue in a heartwarming place of our choosing.

And thank you to Alyssa Baskam, a very special friend, for persevering in editing my tortuous English. Thank you.

I. *"So, in the yeare of our Lord God, 1598, I was hired for chiefe Pilot of a Fleete of five sayle, whiche was made readie by the chiefe of the Indian Company Peter Vanderbag, and Hance Vanderneke; the Generall of this Fleet was a Marchatt called Jaques Mayhay, in which ship, being Admirall, I was Pilot."*[1]

When William Adams, his brother Thomas, and other English pilots and shipmates arrived in Rotterdam they may not have been entirely clear on their intended route to the Far East, nor their ultimate destination within the general area of the Spice Islands. But they knew that this fabled archipelago had been exploited by the Portuguese since 1513 for its highly desired spice products of nutmeg, cloves, and mace, all of which grew in no other place. The three best-known islands were the Sultanates of Tidore and Ternate in the Molucca Sea and Ambon in the nearby Banda Sea. Situated to the south of the Philippines (then known as Spanish Luzon), and west of New Guinea, the whole archipelago was generally referred to as the Moluccas. They are now the provinces of Maluka Utara and Maluka, in Indonesia.

As they made slow but steady preparations for the voyage it must have been frustrating to hear of the departure of other expeditions from the nearby port of Middleburg. Although there are no monsoon seasons in North-Western Europe, most sailors knew that a spring departure offered the best chance to catch the prevailing winds which would facilitate a speedy passage to the Southern seas. By mid-March, 1598, two Dutch flotillas (one of three ships and the other of only two) had embarked for the Spice Islands. Both were smaller than the fleet that would carry William and Thomas Adams.

The latter of the Middleburg flotillas was commanded by Cornelius de Houtman, veteran leader of the 'First Dutch expedition' to have sailed in 1595, and was guided by the Englishman, John Davis, as chief pilot. Davis would have been well-known (if not personally) to William Adams because he was regarded as perhaps the foremost English explorer of the age[2]. He had even written a most valuable treatise for navigators, called *The Seaman's Secrets*, published in 1594, which described for the first time a new device to find latitude known as the Davis Quadrant or, simply, the backstaff. Designed to give an accurate reading in all 90 degrees of latitude, it enabled the navigator to take readings without having to look directly at the sun. It is certain Adams would have carried his own (perhaps slightly modified) version of this instrument since the journey ahead involved travel through the lower latitudes nearest the equator where this instrument excelled. Adams would also have brought his astrolabe for nightly celestial observations, his globes, and the rutters (and other charts) he had compiled or collected over time. He may have also brought his own compass, a set of dividers, and the rulers he required to plot progress during deep-blue ocean voyages.

On 1st May, 1598, another expedition bound for the East Indies set sail from the island of Texel, in the northern part of the Netherlands. Comprising eight ships and backed by the *Onde Compagnie* - essentially the same group of investors who had funded Houtman's 1595 voyage - this venture has now become known as the 'Second Dutch Expedition to Indonesia'. Unknown at the time, of course, it was to be an enormously successful enterprise, returning 400% profit to the shareholders. Under the command of Jacob Cornelius van Neck, the voyage took only three months to reach the Cape of Good Hope and then another four months to reach Bantam, in Java, where four ships were promptly filled to the gunnels with pepper and spices[3]. They were already on their way back to Amsterdam shortly after New Year in 1599 and returned safely in July that year to a tumultuous welcome from the gleeful merchants and citizens of the city. The rest of the fleet made it to the isle of Ambon, returning full of spices the following year. The Dutch golden-age did, at that time, truly get underway.

Meanwhile, in Rotterdam, the Indian Company Adams had signed up to had purchased five ships - all of them used but proven to be sea-worthy. The *Liefde*, for example, had previously sailed under the name *Erasmus*, and carried a figure of the scholar-philosopher as its sternpost. During re-fitting, one thing would have become obvious to any seasoned mariner waiting to board and stow his kit-bag; the ships were being armed as if for war. This was to be no ordinary trading expedition. Compared to the moderately-armed merchant ships Adams had been used to sailing, the ships being equipped for this journey had a greater tonnage and were being set-up for larger cannon (and more of them). The Company - known to financiers as the Rotterdam Company - had been actively lobbying the Holland State Government (the States General) as well as various city-state governments including Rotterdam and Amsterdam, for the loan of large ships' cannon; particularly demi-culverins (which fired 8lb [3.6 kg] shot), or greater (Barreveld, 2001; 32-33). It seems that of a total of fourteen acquired this way, at least ten were of the desired large caliber. Of course, these would complement the usual range of cannon typically carried on each ship.

The ships being fitted were the *Hoop*, the admiral-ship of the fleet, with a capacity of 500-600 tons and an armament of 34 guns; the *Liefde*, the vice-admiral-ship, at 300-400 tons and 18 guns; *Het Geloof*, also 300-400 tons, and 20 guns; the *Trouw*, 250 tons and 16 guns; and finally the *Blijde Boodschap* which was described as a yacht (fast sail-boat) but which still had a 150-ton capacity and was armed with 19 guns[4]. Small-arms were also carried in large numbers. According to a manifest recorded by Jesuit priests after the arrival of the *Liefde* in Japan, the ship carried five hundred muskets; five thousand cast-iron shot; and fifty quintals of gunpowder (approximately 2,500 - 3,000 kilograms). These numbers may be exaggerated since the Jesuits wished to portray the surviving crew as pirates, but the existence of a large quantity of such firearms could not be denied. Given that the crew of the *Liefde* was estimated to be only 110 men at the time of departure from Rotterdam, it seems that many of the side-arms were carried as a trade item. But, of course, any number of them could be utilized by the crew in the event of trouble.

The problem of increasing the offensive/defensive capacity of any ship was the extra space such armament required. The stowage space needed for both trade items and victuals would be compromised by taking on extra cannon. Given the interests of the mercantile and financial backers of the expedition it was more likely to be storage space for food and drink which suffered. The solution would be to regularly re-victual en route to the Far East, using aggression, if necessary, against any enemy shipping encountered. For any such ship the aim would not necessarily be restricted to stealing trade goods or other valuables, but also to rob the defeated crew of their food and water. In fact, it was becoming increasingly clear to observers that the objective of the Rotterdam Company was to emulate Drake's extraordinarily successful voyage of circumnavigation some twenty years earlier. That expedition had stopped six Spanish and Portuguese ships off the African coast and, even after arriving at the Cape Verde islands, had chased-down another Spanish vessel which yielded "victuals … an astrolabe, sailing directions for Brazil, and – more valuable still – a Portuguese pilot … experienced in the voyage between Europe and South America and the owner of several nautical charts" (Sugden, 2006; 103). Again, following in Drake's wake, this Dutch expedition would be more than sufficiently equipped to fight potentially valuable Spanish prize-ships and raid Spanish townships on the Pacific coast of South America.

There was one other item the fleet awaited before the expedition could sail. Each ship was to have possession of a brand-new set of three maps by Dutch cartographers which represented the most up-to-date knowledge of the shape of the world, as defined nation by nation. These were really catalan maps, or sea-charts, drawn on parchment, each representing part of the world on a two-dimensional flat plane. Super-imposed on the shape of the various coastlines on each chart were sixteen compass roses arranged in a circle, all with lines radiating from their centres drawn through the sixteen cardinal points (N; NNE; NE; ENE; E; etc.). The maps also had graduated scales running from top to bottom (north to south) and left to right (west to east) marking off degrees of latitude and longitude respectively.

Two of the charts in each set represented the hemi-spheres - more or less. One, the 'Atlantic chart', showed a truncated England and the Netherlands at the very top of the sheet (Rotterdam *was* included), and the Mediterranean Sea as far as Tripoli, Corsica, and Sardinia (Fig. 1). The whole of the African Atlantic coastline was shown, with about one hundred major ports or coastal settlements clearly labelled. The name 'Africa' was also marked in much larger print. On the other side of the Atlantic the chart displayed both the east and west coasts of South and Central America and the eastern sea-board of North America, which was labelled Terra Florida. South of the equator the names Peru, Bresilien, Chile, and America were written in large print, with the names of many ports and settlements in much smaller print along the coasts. The whole of the course of the Amazon River was shown, but greatly exaggerated in scale to the extent that it appeared to almost bisect the continent.

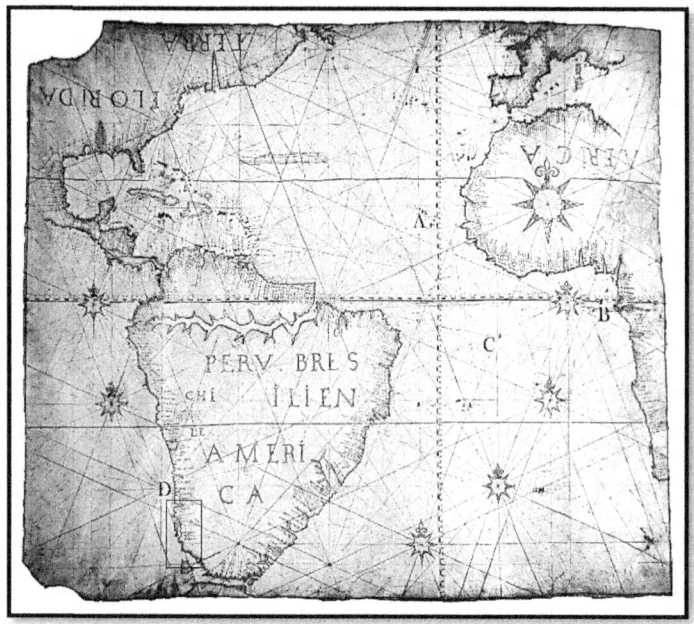

Figure 1. The 'Atlantic Chart' carried aboard the **Liefde**.

    KEY   *A: The Cape Verde Islands*

              B: The general area of the Isle of Annobon, Cape Lopez, and the Manicongo coast

              C: Ascension Island

D: *The general area of the Isles of Mocha and Santa Maria*

The rectangle below 'D' shows the area highlighted in Figure 6.

The second of the hemi-sphere charts might well be called the 'Indian Ocean chart' (Fig. 2). It showed the east-African coastline, the Arabian Peninsula (and the courses of the Tigris and Euphrates Rivers), the Indian sub-continent, the East-Asian continental coastline (including the Malay Peninsula) to China, and a rather vaguely defined Korea. The Philippine and Indonesian archipelagos were also shown in some detail, but there was no hint of Terra Australis. The three southernmost Japanese islands were depicted in the top right-hand segment of the map. No large print names were provided, but ports and coastal settlements were shown in detail along each coast, as with the 'Atlantic chart'. The Pacific Ocean was barely represented at all, indicating the lack of knowledge of this area by Dutch cartographers (and most others) at that time. The actual date of these maps is open to question. Neither one (and they are clearly a pair) had a *cartouche* which would typically display the name of the cartographer and the place and date of publication. In fact, inspection of the compass roses reveals the maps were unfinished because the typical artistic embellishments usually associated with these were obviously incomplete. It would seem the sponsors of the voyage were so keen for the expedition to embark (they were already late) that they were happy to receive the charts as soon as all the 'essential' features had been drawn, foregoing the usual final flourishes.

The third chart, in contrast, was complete (Fig. 3). It showed part of the western Pacific Ocean, drawn to a larger –

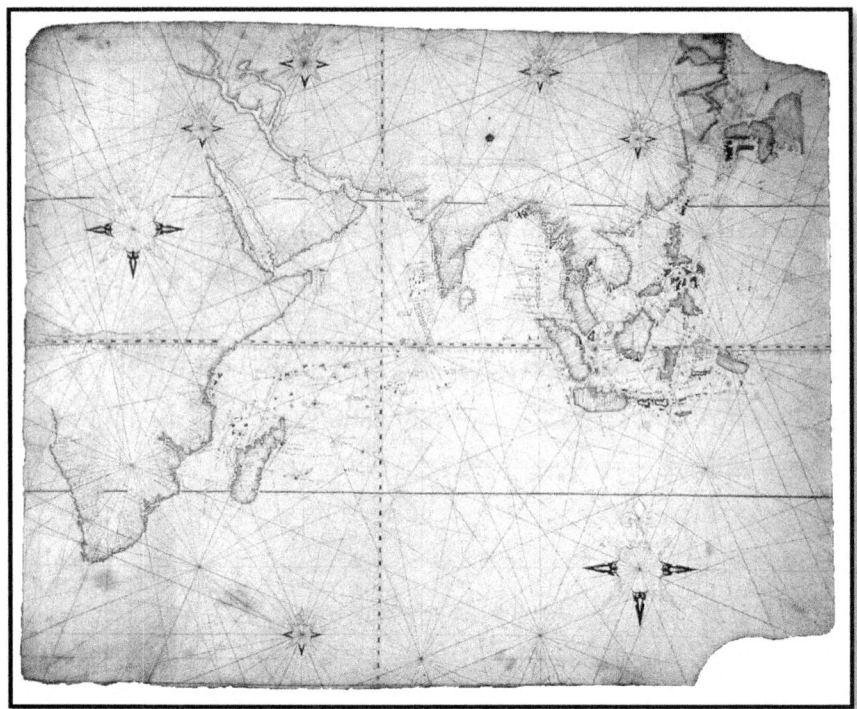

Figure 2. The 'Indian Ocean Chart' carried aboard the Liefde

more detailed – scale than the other maps, highlighting Japan; the Chinese, Cambodian and Siamese coastlines; the Philippines, Borneo, Java, and Nova Guinea; and, filling the southern edge of the chart, Terra Australis. This would be the chart used for navigating to the Spice Islands, although there was no 'accurate' longitudinal scale shown. In the top-left corner of the map was the description (in translation): "compiled by Cornelis Doedsz, of Edam, February 1598". We know this because, remarkably, the three charts supplied to the *Liefde* have all survived and are

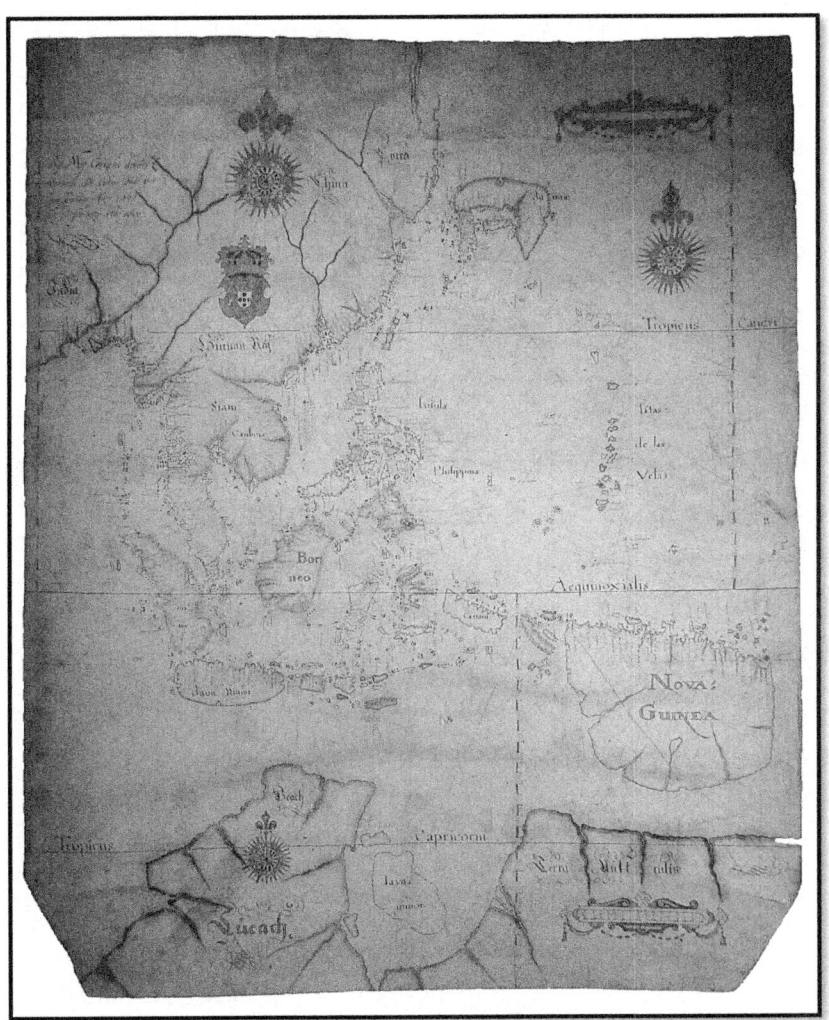

Figure 3. The 'West Pacific Chart' carried aboard the Liefde.

currently held in the Tokyo National Museum. They were acquired by the Museum in the early twentieth century as part of the extensive Tokugawa family collection, part of which was handed-over to the national archive, housed at the then Imperial Museum.

Despite the lack of accreditation for the two hemi-sphere maps they almost certainly belong to the same set of three. This can be known because of the errors shown. Most significantly, the depiction of the passage through the Magellan Strait on the Atlantic Chart is mistaken. One of the few successes of the Mahu expedition was the drawing of an accurate depiction of the Magellan Strait by Jan Outghersz, navigator on the *Het Geloof* (Wieder, 1924; Vol. 2)[5]. His ship returned to Rotterdam in 1600 after failing to make headway across the Pacific, and all subsequent Dutch maps would make use of this information and display a more accurate representation of the Strait. The inaccurate reflection of the Magellan Strait on the Atlantic Chart suggests it and its companion must have been produced for the 1598 Rotterdam Company expedition.

A second major error unifying the three maps was the mis-shape of the islands of Japan. The Japanese islands were depicted in a distinctive 'shrimp' shape – with a large (actually non-existent) promontory shown extending to the south (the 'South Cape'), even beyond the latitude of southern Kyushu. This had been based on the very earliest Portuguese maps of Japan (as seen by Linschoten in Goa[6]). Unlike the Atlantic Chart however, this mistake was not due to the unavailability of information of the time. Even by the early 1590s this representation of Japan had been superseded by more accurate depictions based on the accounts of travels of Jesuit priests to all parts of the mainland and larger islands. Indeed, a skilled Portuguese cartographer named Moreira had been to Japan twice, in 1584-85 and 1590-92, and taken his own measurements. He sent his observations to a friend in Lisbon named Teixeira, who then worked in open collaboration with the Dutch map-maker Ortelius to produce a new and much improved map of Japan (with a greatly fore-shortened 'South Cape'), published in 1595 (Hubbard, 2012; 50-51).

In fact, none of the charts provided by the Company for the *Liefde* were, in the strictest sense, drawn using the very latest information. The problem for the financiers of the Rotterdam Company was that they had no idea what Japan really looked like. The Indian Ocean and the West Pacific charts are both clearly based on the charts produced by van Linschoten in the mid-1590s (Schilder, 2017; 354). Very likely they consulted Dirck van Gerritsz, the only known Dutchman to have ever visited Japan, and who would join their forthcoming expedition, to advise them of the best version. Since he was an old friend of Linschoten it seems he chose that one in preference to the chart by Ortelius, which would ultimately make it exceedingly difficult for William Adams and the crew of the *Liefde* to actually locate Japan, when they found themselves in Japanese waters many months later. It would have given Adams no comfort at all to learn that at the very same time he was looking for the supposed 'South Cape' in 1600, Doedsz – the map compiler – was revising his sea-chart of Japan and the East Indies to depict Japan as Ortelius had done rather than rely on Linschoten's version.

Despite the errors in the *Liefde* charts the investors who commissioned them regarded the information they contained as top-secret and placed great value on them. The allocation of a set of three charts per ship seems to have been normal at the time (Schilder, 2017; 354), and it was expected they should be returned at the end of each voyage. Later, when the various groups of investors had joined to form the Dutch East India Company (VOC) in 1602, and rules were formalized, it became the policy that if any captain failed to give back the Company charts upon the ships' return, he would be fined the equivalent of twice their value (Guleij and Gerrit (eds.), 2017; 19). Whatever their value, the *Liefde* sea-charts were destined never to return to Rotterdam (except in the form of photographic copies, which were sent from the former Imperial Museum in Tokyo to the Rotterdam Maritime Museum in the 1930s. (Those copies were subsequently published in Keuning, 1940; Charts VI-VIII in Appendix LXXI).

Once all the charts were stowed on board (in their generally unfinished state) the expedition was at last ready to sail. Adams stepped off Dutch soil for the last time, probably on 24th

June, to board the *Hoop*, the admiral-ship, as pilot. He was joined on deck by his old friend and circumnavigator Timothy Shotten, who is described as chief-pilot and who, having sailed with Sir Thomas Cavendish on his successful round-the-world expedition in 1588, was probably the only crew member with first-hand experience of the Magellan Strait. There were two other English pilots on board, Thomas Spring and a Master Estrique (probably Stracey, Estrique being a Spanish version of the name)[7], and one Dutch navigator, Pieter Jansz. Later in the voyage some officers, including William Adams, were transferred to other ships as circumstances dictated, and others were moved to the *Hoop*. Thomas Adams, William's younger brother, took up his berth on the *Liefde*, along with Dirck Gerritz Pomp (who had formerly been a gunner, but was now referred to as pilot) and another Dutch navigator, Paulus Hartog (Wieder, 1923; Vol.1, 62-63).

The expedition was commanded by the Admiral: Jacques (or Jacob) Mahu, a young and popular merchant who would look after the interests of the Company on the voyage. His role was really more administrator than sailor, and he had been appointed to his command because of his mercantile rather than maritime skills. He was the same age as William Adams, having also been born in 1564. Indeed, the vice-admiral and all the other captains were also aged in their thirties. The oldest, at 39-years, was the vice-admiral and commander of the *Liefde*, seigneur Simon de Cordes. Like seigneur Gerrit van Beuningen, the 38-year-old captain of *Het Geloof*, the pair were experienced merchant-adventurer minor aristocrats, accustomed to positions of command. Youngest of the captains was 30-year-old Jeuriaen de Bockholt of the *Trouw*. Also from a merchant family he was a sickly young man, possibly suffering tuberculosis, who may have been encouraged to go to sea to improve his health (Barreveld, 2001; 42). The only experienced mariner among the commanders was Sebald de Weert, captain of the yacht *Blijd Boodschap*, who was aged 31-years. With all the captains now aboard their respective ships, the fleet finally departed Rotterdam on 27th June, 1598.

II. *"**Loving Wife, you shall understand how all things have passed with me from the time of mine absence from you. We set saile with five ships from the Texel in Holland the four and twentieth of June, 1598. And departed the Coast of England the fift of July."***

These few simple lines were written by William Adams to his wife in 1605 (Purchas, 1625; Vol. 3, 129). It seems almost incomprehensible that so many inaccuracies exist, but they do. For example, it is well-known that the expedition of which he was a member departed from the city of Rotterdam on the River Meuse, and not the Island of Texel which lay many miles to the north. In fact, the first official account of the initial stages of the voyage had been published in 1600 - five years before Adams' letter. It was compiled by a publisher named Zacharias Heyns, a close friend of Captain Sebald de Weert who had led the *Het Geloof* back to the port at Rotterdam in July that year. Heyns' primary source was a journal kept by the surgeon aboard the *Het Geloof*, called Barnard Jansz, although the notes and recollections of de Weert and other sailors from the ship were also used (Barreveld, 2001; 44-45). Hereafter, this publication is referred to as Sebald de Weert's journal, although a more accurate title would be the 'Journal of the Voyage of Sebald de Weert'. According to this account, the fleet set sail in good order on 27th June, 1598 – backed by a north-easterly breeze. Then the wind died, leaving them off the English coast near the Kent port of Deal, where they were forced to wait until 15th July for a favourable wind to blow again (Wieder, 1923; Vol.1, 148). It is possible, of course, that the simple passage of time had clouded Adams' memory. But errors and inconsistencies (regarding dates especially) appear throughout the letter penned to his wife in 1605; so many indeed as to suggest other explanations may be appropriate.

The discrepancy concerning the date of departure is probably the easiest to explain. Some years later, in a letter to 'Unknown Friends and Countrymen', Adams stated that it was 23rd or 24th June that the expedition set sail (Purchas, 1625; Bk.3, 125). There were several occasions in the second letter where, in the same manner, and perhaps because of the longer passage of time, Adams is a little vague when describing a precise date. But Adams is at least consistent between his own accounts in this instance, and he believed departure was a few days earlier than Captain de Weert stated. The reason was clearly due to a simple mis-understanding. Adams recalls the time he *boarded* ship from the quay, for the last time, ready to cast-off. Shortly after, the ship was towed by pinnace to the roads(tead) at Rotterdam to await a suitable wind and tide for final departure. It was at this moment, while waiting at anchor on the River Meuse, that a drawing was made of the fleet (shown under sail), later used to illustrate Heyns' publication (Schilder, 2017; 352)[8]. This account was correct in describing the date of *final* departure as 27th June, when the fleet departed the roads at Rotterdam.

The ten-day discrepancy in the date of departure from the English coast has a different explanation. The delay at the English coast was a situation Adams would have been familiar with. He must have known the port of Deal well, having been held up at the Downs on more than one occasion in the past, and would have known all the inns and taverns there[9]. Having the sense and knowledge of the signs indicating when the wind was likely to change, he could afford to relax in the company of friends and other mariners who happened to be stuck there as well. Indeed, he could switch back to an English rather than Dutch style of life and way of thinking, including use of the 'old-style' Julian calendar instead of the 'new-style' Gregorian calendar adopted by the Dutch[10]. There was a difference between the two calendars of ten days. To an Englishman a date such as the 20th day of the month would be, to a Dutchman, the 30th. To English protestants, Pope Gregory had apparently 'lost' ten days in the story of the Universe – and, by extension, the record of passage of the Sun, the Earth, the Moon, the planets, and the stars through the astronomical calendar – a difficult concept for *all* navigators to accept, irrespective of nationality and religious conviction. In an English/old-fashioned/Julian frame of mind departure from the English coast would have occurred on the 5th July, ten days 'earlier' than a departure date of the 15th July as recorded by Sebald de Weert, who followed the Gregorian dictum. But, by the same logic, Adams should have recorded boarding the ship at Rotterdam to have occurred on 14th June (OS), as opposed to 24th

June (NS). It is clear that in his first letter home, in particular, Adams does occasionally confuse the two calendars, perhaps, as in this instance, relying on the dates which had become stuck in his mind based on the different surrounds he found himself in.

An additional explanation for the discrepancies is that when writing to his wife, six or seven years after the events he recounts, he was, by that time, fully conversant with the Gregorian calendar, but was writing to someone only familiar with the Julian style. In other words, he may have attempted to convert dates as he wrote them into the Julian calendar, simply for her benefit. However, resorting to an English way of thinking proved to be difficult from time to time. Adding ten days when converting Gregorian to Julian, or subtracting ten days if *vice-versa*, may seem simple enough, but it becomes complicated when extended over months of unequal length (28 days; 30 days; or 31 days). And further, the logic of adding days for an event that 'already happened' on the other calendar is not always clear – in anyone's mind. Confusion will happen, and major mistakes can be made, resulting in the date which is actually written being twenty days different from the date that was intended (if ten days are subtracted instead of added, for instance). At least the letter to his wife is consistent in its inconsistencies. The missive is generally written with reference to the Julian calendar, but sometimes the date (for example, boarding ship in Rotterdam) refers to the Gregorian system and, occasionally, a major mistake is made – confusing everyone.

The irony is that, as pilot, the accurate recording of time, and date, was of the utmost importance. Having finally left England's shores, Adams soon became immersed in the new-style calendar[11]. It is interesting to note that Adams usually only refers to precise dates when describing the events of his voyage to Japan, or in ship's logs that he kept on other voyages made towards the end of his life. To an extent, imprecision may be acceptable given the period and the nature of Adams' constraints, but when certain dates enter the history books with regularity, such as the date of Adams' arrival in Japan, it is good to identify the exact date with as much clarity and as little confusion as possible. Adams letters are the only accounts which survive for the *whole* of the voyage, but they can be compared to Sebald de Weert's account, or fragmentary Spanish and Japanese sources where episodes coincide. A comparative table of dates describing the voyage is presented in the Appendix.

The issue of contradictory dates, as well as other apparent falsehoods in Adams' accounts, can be considered from yet one more perspective. As with access to the maps and charts, the Dutch tended to be very secretive regarding the exact course followed by their expeditions. It is likely for this reason that Adams was encouraged by his erstwhile captain, Jacob Quaeckernaeck, who would also be the bearer of the letter to his wife, to offer a misleading clue regarding the origin of the expedition[12]. If, by chance, the letter fell into Portuguese or

Spanish hands, they might be confused if the voyage was described as having departed Texel instead of Rotterdam. Indeed, it seems the Dutch did not want some of the content of Adams' first letter to be seen even by English eyes. As Purchas notes at the end of his transcript of the letter: "The rest of this letter, by the malice of the bearers, was suppressed…" (Purchas, 1625; Bk.3, 132).

III. *"…the Pilots should be no more in the Councell…"*[13]

The delay of several days of the voyage through the English Channel was frustrating, especially to seasoned mariners who knew that the best chance to catch the desired easterly winds would have meant a departure in March or April. Even though the fault for loss of time lay with the sponsors and organizers of the expedition, the onus would be on the captains and pilots to make-up time later in the voyage whenever favourable winds or currents presented themselves. Having departed Deal (or, more accurately, The Downs) on 15th July, Adams thought nothing was worth recording of the early stages of the voyage until the expedition neared the Cape Verde Islands, six weeks later. He merely noted, rather drily, that "… it was somewhat too late ere we came to the Line (i.e., the Equator), to passe it without contrarie winds" (Purchas, 1625; Vol. 3, 125).

The journal of Captain de Weert, on the other hand, recounts several incidents in the first few weeks of the expedition which offer important clues to how the fleet was organized. Additionally, there are a few contemporary sketches of the fleet to indicate the order in which they normally sailed (Fig. 4). Figure 4a shows the fleet in the Rotterdam Roads on the River Meuse as it was about to set sail on 27th June. The illustration identifies each ship, clearly showing the admiral's flag atop the mainmast of the

Figure 4a. At the Rotterdam Roads, prior to departure

Figure 4b. The fleet enters the southern Pacific Ocean

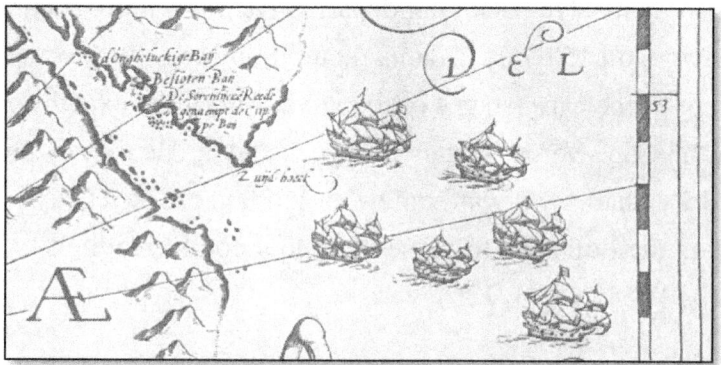

Figure 4. These contemporary depictions of the Mahu fleet were published after the return of Het Geloof *to Rotterdam in July, 1600. In Fig.4b the positioning of the admiral's flags suggests the usual sailing order was for the* Hoop *to lead the fleet and the* Liefde *to follow at the rear.*

Hoop and a similar flag atop the *foremast* of the *Liefde*, indicating the ship's vice-admiral status. The sketch in Figure 4b shows the last occasion the fleet were all together, leaving the Magellan Strait on 3rd September, 1599. The *Hoop* and the *Liefde* can be identified because of the depiction of the admiral's flags; the *Hoop* leading the fleet out of the Strait, and the *Liefde* at the rear keeping the fleet together. This was likely to have been the general order of sailing throughout the progress of the expedition. Approaching coastal areas, however, the yacht *Blijd Boodschap* probably would have been sent ahead to act as scout, looking out for hidden reefs or shallow sandbanks. A sixth ship is also shown in Fig. 4b, being the smallest in the fleet. It is the ship's pinnace from the *Hoop*, called the *Postillion*, which followed the *Hoop* out of the Strait but shortly afterwards sank without trace in a storm.

The mood among the crews in the early days of the expedition was certainly good, for the quantity of daily rations that were issued seemed to exceed their best expectations (Milton, 2002; 64). Of course, such liberal disbursement of the stores every mealtime could not be sustained, but the admiral and captains seemed content in the knowledge that their combined fire-power would ensure the re-supply of all victuals every time they encountered and captured an 'enemy' vessel, of Spanish, Portuguese, or French origin[14]. According to de Weert's journal, morale was boosted even more when, in the evening of 10th August, a Spanish-style sailing rig was sighted in a fleet of four ships off Cape Saint Vincent, the south-westernmost point of

Portugal.

Admiral Mahu did not hesitate in giving chase, whereupon the 'enemy' split-up, sailing in different directions. The Mahu fleet also split, with the *Hoop,* the *Liefde* and the *Trouw* chasing down the nearest ship. William Adams, who was on board the *Hoop*, would have observed the vessel heave-to after a single cannon shot was fired. By then all must have realized it was, in fact, a friendly English trader they had been pursuing. All the ships carried a pinnace and one was duly lowered from the *Hoop* to send a small party of men across. It is quite possible that Adams, being an Englishman, was sent to parley with the other captain, but he makes no mention of the incident in his letters. As things turned out this friendly fleet comprised both English and Dutch ships, the Dutch having been arrested by the English as suspected smugglers. There was no question of Admiral Mahu taking goods or victuals from them; instead, they took on a few more Dutch sailors who were apparently disaffected with their new English masters (Barreveld, 2001; 48). The unexpected outcomes, therefore, were a few red-faces and more mouths to feed.

Of greater concern was the need to recall the other two ships in the fleet before they disappeared altogether in the fading light. The gunner on the *Hoop* fired another shot as a signal to regroup and, after a short while, the yacht *Blijde Boodschap* turned around to rejoin. The other ship, *Het Geloof*, under the command of Captain Gerrit van Beuningen, carried on sailing into the night despite more signal shots being fired. Eventually the Admiral had to dispatch the *Liefde* and the *Trouw* to chase the chaser, wasting the whole of the night and most of the next day bringing him back (Wieder, 1923; Vol.1, 150).

Captain Gerrit van Beuningen warrants a detailed mention. Aged 38 years, and of north German origin, he was the only member of the Mahu fleet known to have sailed on 'the first Dutch expedition', in 1595 (although it is likely that a few unrecorded mariners were also on that voyage). Not that he would have much useful information to impart; he got into such a furious row with the expedition's leader (Cornelius de Houtman) that he ended-up locked in irons and confined to his cabin for most of the voyage. He never actually set foot in the East Indies and was only released when the ship returned to home-waters more than a year later (Barreveld, 2001; 41). He was arrogant and opinionated; refused to listen to 'superiors' whenever he disagreed with a decision (as the incident off Cape St. Vincent demonstrates); and was generally belligerent - or perhaps *gung-ho* in modern parlance. Sebald de Weert and others on board the *Het Geloof*, on whose journal this account is based, referred to him as 'the General', even though van Beuningen had no known training as either soldier or mariner[15]. There is no record whatsoever of what William Adams thought about him but, as subsequent events unfolded, the feeling must have become one of growing disdain.

It took a day or so for the fleet to join-up, having

dispersed during the chase of the ships just encountered. It was vital to Admiral Mahu that the fleet stayed together from this point, for he was now almost certainly following secret orders drawn up by the Admiralties of the Dutch ports. Even though he might be in need of water and food, he was to avoid detection by authorities in the Portuguese possession of Madeira and the Spanish-controlled Canary Islands at all costs. He is unlikely to have known it, but a major raid (involving more than seventy Dutch warships) on the Isle of Gran Canaria was being planned by the Dutch for the following year, with the aim of securing a base for provisioning future Dutch expeditions to the East Indies. Any contact between the Spanish and the Mahu fleet in this area at this time might have jeopardized those plans[16]. Mahu's orders, therefore, were to sail as close as possible to the African coast, avoiding any potential sighting by Spanish or Portuguese vessels until the Canary Islands were behind them.

All went well for eight days after the Cape St. Vincent incident. Then, at night, *Het Geloof*, which appeared to be leading the fleet, suddenly found itself in danger of shoaling near the Moroccan shoreline. Captain van Beuningen had inadvertently sailed into waters less than five fathoms deep and was forced suddenly to drop anchor. *Blijde Boodschap*, again sailing in consort, anchored in just over seven fathoms while the rest of the fleet spotted the danger and stood-off until dawn. Van Beuningen must have felt the eyes of all the other ships' crews upon him as he struggled to regain position, getting his ropes and anchor cables tangled in the process (Barreveld, 2001; 50). Although no latitudinal position is recorded for this event it almost certainly took place at 28°N, near the narrow gap where the Canaries are closest to the African coast. Running onto the leeward shore, especially at night, was a constant danger. Luckily the fleet avoided serious mishap this time. Nevertheless, it was beholden to the admiral, Jacques Mahu, no doubt urged-on by furious expletives from a fuming Captain van Beuningen, to lay the blame on every pilot. Mahu ordered them to better co-ordinate in future to ensure a more accurate positional fix (ibid.). This appeared to be, in essence, a sensible instruction and would be carried out prior to bi-weekly meetings of the fleet captains.

As the fleet entered tropical waters temperatures rose - in both the figurative and literal sense. Tensions within the ship's crews clearly began to emerge at this time. It was not just the growing universal debate about whether the captains or the pilots should oversee setting a course for the ship on a day-by-day basis, though this likely played a significant role in generating friction. The pilots felt that as the 'master mariners' they could best interpret the vagaries of winds, tides, and ocean currents, and the set of the sails, and so fix a safe course for all on board. To them, for the greater part, the ship's captains were the mere spawn of wealthy aristocrats, ignorant of maritime affairs, who had been appointed, perhaps anointed, to command the comings and goings of all aspects of each ship. On this expedition, apart from Captain De Weert, who was a mariner, other captains could only command the respect of the pilots if they demonstrated an understanding of the basics of navigation based on personal experience or were at least sufficiently diplomatic to listen to a pilot's thoughts before making any decision. As far as the captains were concerned, their responsibility was to the investors who appointed them, and who expected trade to be conducted in the most expeditious and profitable manner possible. The captain's orders outweighed all others, therefore, even if it did mean a disagreement with the navigators about the best course to set. This debate continued for centuries. It could and often did create festering wounds - only healed by bonds of personal friendships and mutual understanding.

The forging of such bonds was often hampered, however, by national differences. Although the Englishmen and Dutchmen shared a mutual dislike of the Spanish and Portuguese, this did not mean that the two sets of nationals necessarily got on together. The English may have felt a sense of superiority over their Dutch comrades because they had developed the skills required for global circumnavigation, whereas the Dutch were (to them) mere fishers of herring. Moreover, the English had defeated the Spanish in a decisive naval battle and, in so doing, had helped the Dutch towards liberation of the Spanish Netherlands from Spanish rule. A certain degree of deference and gratitude was doubtless expected.

The Dutch, on the other hand, knew that it was they who had the resources and fortitude to fund expeditions to the faraway oceans, on a scale that had the potential to reap huge profits. It was they who could produce the charts to find those treasures and it was they, as representatives of the financial sponsors, who were ultimately in charge. It did not help that the pilots aboard *Het Geloof* were Dutchmen, while those on the ships which avoided potential disaster on the Moroccan coast were mostly English. John Davis, the English navigator on one of the other Dutch expeditions at this time, noted in his diaries several instances where there was friction between Dutch and English elements of the crew of the ship in which he was master-mariner. As he pointed out, the general feeling amongst the Dutch captains was that "the English were to be thrust in a corner" (Egerton, 1934; 754).

Provisions and waning health also contributed to crew tensions. Even though the fleet had been sailing for only five weeks since leaving the Downs, profligate helpings at mealtimes now meant that food and water supply was becoming a problem. The admiral had no option except to order that the daily intake be rationed by halving the bread allowance. As a result, scurvy began to appear and several crew members died. It became vital that they stop to re-provision at the next archipelago on their route south – the Cape Verde islands, which lay fourteen degrees north of the equator. These islands were under the control of the Portuguese and potentially unfriendly but, since the Dutch were in theory vassals of the Spanish crown (which now controlled all Portuguese affairs) a cautious, if not polite reception could be expected. After all, this fleet was made up of 'peaceful traders' who had shown absolutely no animosity to any Spanish or Portuguese ship during their mission. They would not mention, of course, that this lack of animus was more a matter of bad luck than good judgement! It was also felt that if the Portuguese displayed any suspicion, the fleet would be strong enough to enforce re-supply of victuals by arms if necessary.

The Isle of Santa Iago was sighted on 31st August. Mahu was cautious in his approach, sailing around the island before dispatching all fleet pinnaces to Praya Bay, where he had noted two small European ships at anchor. Navigation was difficult and held-up progress of the fleet, particularly when the winds were contrary. The result was that the local inhabitants had plenty of forewarning of the Dutch presence and fled, so that when the Dutch boarded the two ships, they found them to be deserted and empty of useful items. The ships were seized anyway and made a part of the Dutch fleet for use as store ships.

The only Portuguese presence on this part of the island was a small garrison in a hill-top fort, who fired at the Dutch with a cannon shot or two and sent-off a messenger to warn the governor who was on another part of the island. At this point 'the General' – Captain van Beuningen – persuaded Admiral Mahu to dispatch 150 marines and armed Dutch sailors, with himself in command, to capture the fort. They marched to the beat of drums and the blaring of trumpets, occupying a small chapel on their way up the hill-side from where they fired a volley of shots. The defenders fled, and the fort was soon taken and occupied. Sixty Dutch reinforcements were called, but the fort provided no stores, no food, and no water; only three cannon which they could use to defend themselves – against a handful of bemused locals. The next day a Portuguese magistrate came peacefully, with a message from the governor. Why, he asked, if the Dutch had come with good intent, did they resort to stealing two ships; occupying a place of worship; and storming the fort? The Dutch captains replied that 'needs must' because they were so short of supplies, but that they had genuinely arrived with peaceful intent. The magistrate offered to deliver this message to the governor – and another day was wasted.

It is no surprise that the governor prevaricated as much as he could; he knew that he was probably out-manned and certainly out-gunned by the Mahu fleet. In fact, protracted discussions continued for some days by means of letters carried between the admiral and the governor by a Dutch cabin-boy who could speak Portuguese (Barreveld, 2001; 54). Mahu was still hampered by contrary winds at this stage and could not sail the larger ships in his fleet to São Iago where the governor had his residence. Nor, for that matter, could the ships bring their guns to bear on the small town to threaten the governor. Making things worse, the local climate was considered unwholesome, and many of the crews on all the ships were falling sick, including the admiral and, almost certainly, William Adams himself. Many of the pilots began to argue the case for leaving Cape Verde but, as Adams later noted:

"… the reason that we abode so long at these Ilands was that one of the Captaines of our Fleet made our Generall believe that at these Ilands we should find great store of refreshing, as goats and other things which was untrue" (Purchas, 1625, Bk.3; 130).

Almost certainly this was Captain van Beuningen, who had travelled this area in 1596 with the First Expedition – before being locked-up.

A General Council was called, which was attended by all senior officers, including the navigators, as well the admiral, vice-admiral, and the three other captains. The pilots stated their collective opinion that the fleet should leave immediately, if not for the sickness already infesting the ships, then for the sake of reaching the Magellan Strait before the summer season ended in the southern hemisphere. Captain van Beuningen forcefully laid-out his case that victuals were to be found on the islands, and that the fleet should stay until supplies had been secured. He won the argument but, more than that, venting his spleen at the English pilots he ensured that navigators should no longer attend General Council meetings. As Adams recorded events in the letter to his wife:

"Here I and all the Pilots of the fleet were called to a Councell:

in which wee all shewed our judgements of disliking the place: which were by all the Captaines taken so ill, that afterward it was agreed by them all, that the Pilots should be no more in the Councell, the which was executed." (ibid.)

This was, of course, a grave error of judgement, for the captains were formally excluding, or deliberately ignoring, the advice of highly experienced mariners who would guide the fleet through some of the most dangerous waters on the planet. In the end, the fleet left the Isle of Santa Iago, without reaching any agreement for re-supply with the governor. They sailed for the nearby Isle of Brava where Admiral Mahu had to resort to sending his pinnaces into sheltered bays in search of water and whatever food their crews could pillage. They were successful in obtaining a few barrels of water, some millet, and turtle eggs, but this was by no means sufficient to replenish the whole fleet (Barreveld, 2001; 58-60). And no further substantial supplies were secured at the Cape Verde islands.

IV.   *"...and many of our men were sick..."*[17]

After twenty-four days mostly wasted at the Cape Verde islands the Mahu expedition departed on 15th September, sailing on a south-easterly course with the trade wind blowing from the north-east (Barreveld, 2001; 61). They were headed for the African rather than South American coast, because at 14°N the ocean currents here favoured good progress to be made in the general direction of the equator, albeit in a south-easterly rather than south-westerly direction. Later, this proved to have been a fundamental error of judgement, perhaps caused by lack of suitable consultation with the pilots. A better course at this stage would have been to head south-west. In any case, there were plenty of mitigating factors to explain why the desire for speed of progress at this stage should be considered more important than accuracy of direction. The hold had not been fully replenished with victuals and the rate of sickness was growing rapidly. Not only was the admiral sick and his condition becoming worse daily, but many other officers aboard the *Hoop* had also succumbed to contagious disease, including William Adams. The desire seems to have been to get across the equator first, and then chose a specific location to head towards for nourishment and resuscitation.

As the admiral's condition continued to worsen, command was passed to the vice-admiral, Simon de Cordes, who immediately ordered that three or four of the sickest men on the

Hoop be moved to other ships and replaced with healthy crew. Although not stated explicitly, it would seem he was directing the transfer of the *officers* who were falling ill, which explains William Adams' transfer to the *Liefde* at this time in exchange for the Dutch pilot Paulus Hartog (Wieder, 1923; Vol.1, 165). It is certainly plausible that de Cordes considered Thomas Adams to be the best person to take care of his sick elder brother and that together they could somehow rotate watch duties.

The admiral passed away during the night of 23rd September, and three hours later his clerk died too. Just four days after that Pieter Jansz, one of the other sick pilots aboard *De Hoop*, also died. At a solemn ceremony held aboard ship on 25th September, Jacques Mahu's coffin was carried from stem to stern in full-view of the whole fleet, and then lowered beneath the waves. After the funeral a General Council was convened. A sealed-package, containing secret orders for this eventuality, was opened and vice-admiral Simon de Cordes was formally named and lauded as the new commander of the fleet. Captain van Beuningen became vice-admiral and the vacancy for a new captaincy was awarded to the seasoned Dirck van Gerritsz. As admiral, de Cordes would move from the *Liefde* to the flagship, the *Hoop*, and his former cabin would become occupied by van Beuningen. Seebald de Weert was to be transferred to take command of *Het Geloof,* and van Gerritsz to the yacht *Blijde Boodschap*. Captain Jeuriaen van Bockholt, in command of the *Trouw* and who was also gravely ill, remained in place (Barreveld,

2001; 63). Before any of these transfers took place, however, de Cordes instructed each captain to count the remaining food and water supplies on his ship. De Cordes was, literally, taking stock of their general situation, and it did not look good.

According to Adams: "…we came to the Line (ie. the equator) …about the midst of September…" and Admiral Mahu died "…in the latitude of three degrees to the south (of the equator)…"[18]. Both statements are demonstrably wrong but could be ascribed to simple error if he really meant October instead of September, and 3° north instead of 3° south (similar mistakes occur elsewhere in his manuscripts). It is more likely that these mistakes resulted because Adams was so gravely ill at this time that he had no clear recollection of events as they happened. Even more telling is the absence of any description by him of the near catastrophic sequence of events which overtook the crews during late-September and the whole of October. His failure to remark on them suggests just how grave his condition was, just as the events themselves reflect the navigational befuddlement on the quarterdeck of the flagship and all other ships where senior officers were falling seriously ill.

On the 25th September, the same day as the funeral of Admiral Mahu, the *Blijd Boodschap* made a depth sounding of only 26 fathoms (Wieder, 1923; Vol.1, 167). This indicates the fleet may have been much closer to Africa than intended, although the coast was not quite in sight. A generally southward course was maintained while the captains completed their inventories and then, on 29th September, they transferred ships as their orders had dictated. On that day, Admiral de Cordes reviewed their situation from the *Hoop* and ordered a change of direction to between "south-west by south, and south south-west". Veering westward in this way would seem to indicate that de Cordes still intended to head for the South American coast for revictualling, and this intent seems to have been confirmed when, a few days later, on 4th October, the course was changed again to "west south-west" (ibid.).

Unfortunately, no record survives of the latitude reached at this time, but the relatively good progress made until the end of September would suggest that the fleet had already come close to the "equinoctall line". In fact, the course changes initiated by de Cordes might indicate that he was trying to extract the most benefit from the fading north-easterly trade winds which had brought them this far. They were entering a zone known as the Doldrums, so named for the lack of wind here, and these small navigational changes were meant to steer the fleet as far *south* as possible while any wind remained in this otherwise windless zone.

De Cordes would have been aware of the existence of the Doldrums, and knew it was a relatively narrow belt extending over just a few degrees of latitude. His intent was to get through the zone in as short a time as possible, to reach the trade winds which blew on the other, southern side of the equator. Only then could he expect to regain sufficient strength of wind to allow him to steer to the nearest land for essential revictualling. Just two days later, on 6th October, it seems the fleet was finally becalmed. The admiral ordered a lowering of all ship's boats. They attached cables to the prows of each ship and effected a reversal of direction by towing through oar-power. The fleet was now headed east-south-east again. and pointing towards the African coast (Wieder, 1923; Vol.1, 167). It cannot be known if this was the admiral's intention from the outset, or if he only now realized that the fleet could not make it to the "Brasilien" coast.

The Doldrums occur in an area known today by the much less evocative acronym, "ITCZ" or Inter Tropical Convergence Zone. The position of the zone migrates each year following the apparent north-south seasonal movement of the sun between the Tropics of Cancer and Capricorn. In essence, the zone covers areas of ocean which are closest to the sun and therefore subject to the greatest heat. Surface sea temperatures reach more than 30° centigrade, and sea-water evaporates as the air is forced to rise instead of flowing laterally. The Doldrums are hot, sultry, and, above all, still. The sea takes on a mirror-like quality, and sailors may be entranced into inactivity, not wanting to disturb the illusion of complete tranquility. The fleet had reached this zone in early October, not long after the autumn equinox when the Doldrums straddle the equator. Although there is no mention of this episode in any of the journals or letters which survive, the captains of each ship would have continued deploying their boats so that sailors who were fit enough could tow the ships by rowing in a south or south-easterly direction[19]. Equally important for getting out of the Doldrums, however, were the ocean currents which carried them along, almost unnoticed. De Cordes would have realized he was in the eastward flowing Guinea current, and so had no choice but to head towards the shores of Africa.

Sometime in mid-October the fleet finally crossed the equator, and by the 27th of that month de Weert recorded their position as 1°40' south (ibid.). The wind had finally picked up again, and the admiral ordered prayers to be said in thanksgiving, and for mitigation of the dire circumstances the fleet still found itself in. On 2nd November, de Weert's journal (based on surgeon Barentz Jansz' observations) noted that the state of sickness on all ships was extremely bad, with as many as 70 crew on the *Het Geloot* unfit for duty, and an average of 30 to 40 crew on each of the other ships in a similar state (Wieder, 1923; Vol.1, 168). The urgency now was not just the need for victuals, but to get the sick ashore and healthy again as quickly as possible. Admiral De Cordes ordered another change of direction therefore, this time to the north-east, aiming for the small island of Annobon. This was another Portuguese colony, well-known as a stopping point for ships requiring fresh-water and supplies. It was also the closest land – or so it was thought.

By the next day, 3rd November, the fleet was heading north-east, and re-crossing the parallel at latitude 3°s, but their longitudinal position was a long way from where they believed themselves to be. In part, this may have been because several of the senior pilots, including Adams, were sick and could not contribute to providing an accurate fix of their true position. Continuing tensions between the captains and pilots may also have played a role. The real problem, however, was that in the Doldrums, where everything appeared to be so still, it was difficult to get an accurate estimate of the speed of the current which was still carrying them eastward. In fact, the south-east course the fleet had set since leaving the Cape Verde Islands had brought them into the influence of the fast-moving Guinea current, which flows west to east, and which is strongest where the Atlantic is bounded to the north by the African coast, from modern-day Liberia to Cameroon.

Sailing out of sight of land it was almost impossible to get a true indication of longitude and their rate of progress eastwards. The fleet was only saved from complete disaster when a sharp-eyed lookout on board the *Hoop* during the night of 3rd November noticed surf breaking on the coast ahead. Warning shots were fired to notify the rest of the fleet and all but one of the ships managed to drop anchor in time to prevent them being wrecked. The ship that failed to stop was the larger of the sloops (30-tons) taken on the Isle of Santa Iago in the Cape Verde Islands, with eleven crew aboard. It was lost in the night and never seen again. They had not reached the Isle of Annobon, however, but the continental African coast, a few miles north of the River Congo estuary. All the ships' navigators had miscalculated their longitudinal position, none of them expecting to see land for another 100 or 120 miles. De Weert even suggests that one pilot was wrong by as much as 200 miles (Wieder, 1923; Vol.1, 168).

The fleet had reached a part of the coast they called Manicongo[20], but since the shore proved inaccessible because of the dangerous surf, they sailed north for Capo de Lopo Gonzales (Cape Lopez in modern-day Gabon), where the natives were said to be friendly. It took until 9th November to find a safe anchorage, at the latitude of 0°30's, and that day was spent carrying all the sick crew to the beach to lay them down under hastily constructed shelters, arranged according to ship's companies (Wieder, 1923; Vol.1, 169).

Although fish were in abundance, other local foods were scarce and the local people proved elusive, offering little more than a 'peddling trade' when they did appear. The admiral clearly did not wish to risk moving the sick again, some of whom were extremely ill indeed. After a restful sojourn of almost two weeks, a French trader arrived at the same anchorage and offered to introduce the Dutch to the local chieftain personally. De Weert was ordered to go and negotiate with the 'Negro King', but he returned a few days later with nothing more than a few empty promises from his fickle host to trade provisions for some of the goods the Dutch carried – and many yarns about the strange times he had experienced at the chieftain's palace, which he equated to no more than a cattle-pen. He later recalled that:

> "**Little refreshing was there to be had. A Bore and two Buffals they** [the Dutch] **killed in the Woods; a little they bought, a few Birds they tooke, and (which worse was) as the Scorbuto** [scurvy] **forsooke the sicke, Fevers possessed the stronger.**" (Purchas, 1625; Bk. 2, 79)[21].

Since it was clear that men were now succumbing to fever as quickly as those who had suffered scurvy were recovering, de Cordes determined that there was no longer any point in staying here, and that they should set course once more for the Isle of Annobon[22]. The fleet weighed anchor and departed the "coast of *Gynny*" on 10th December, 1598.

Adams was almost certainly amongst those carried ashore with fever, the symptoms requiring many days to be spent in bed, followed by a long and slow recovery if death was avoided. Obviously he did recover, slowly recuperating during the weeks spent ashore. His account of those days focussed on the sick and is again rather confused regarding his location and dates of arrival and departure. He wrote in his first letter, to his wife:

> "**…we were forced upon the Coast of Guiney, falling upon an head-land called *Cabo de Spiritu Sancta*. The new Generall commanded to beare up with *Cape de Lopo Conzalves*, there to seek refreshing for our men, the which we did. In which place we landed all our sicke men, where they did not much better,**

for wee could find no store of victuals. The nine and twentieth of December, wee set saile to goe on our Voyage; and in our way we fell with an Island called *Illha da Nobon* where we landed all our sicke men, taking the Island in by force. Their towne contayned about eightie houses. Having refreshed our men, we set saile againe." (Purchas, 1625; Bk.3, 130).

Clearly, Adams had not been involved, in any way, with de Cordes' decision to head for Annobon as a destination, and this is confirmed in his second letter, to 'Unknown Friends':

"…we were forced to goe to the Coast of *Gynny* to Cape *de Lopo Gonzalves*, where wee set our sicke men a land, whereof many dyed: and of the sicknesse, few bettered, having little or no refreshing, and the place being unhealthy. Therefore, to fulfill our Voyage, we set our course for the coast of *Brazill*, determining to passe the Straights of *Magellan*, and by the way came to an Island called *Illha da Nobon*, at which Iland we landed, and tooke the towne, which contained about eightie houses, in which Iland we refreshed our selves, having Oxen, Oranges and divers other fruits. But the unwholesomenesse of the Aire was such, that as one bettered, another fell sicke: we spent upon the Coast of the Cape of *Gonzalves*, and of *Annobon* about two moneths time till the twelfth or thirteenth of November. At which time, wee set sayle from *Annobon*…" (Purchas, 1625; Bk.3, 125).

In neither letter do Adams' dates tally with de Weert's cohesive account. Also, unusual for Adams letters, there is a remarkable degree of similarity between the passages cited above, suggesting perhaps that Adams only retained a vague memory of events as they happened here and, when he came to write them down, had to rely on the reminiscences of a third party who had shared the experience, such as Melchior van Santvoort, or Jacob Quaeckernaeck.

According to de Weert, it took only a few days of sailing to reach Annobon, a small island with one central mountain. The fleet presumably followed accurate bearings obtained with the help of the friendly French trader they had recently encountered. With the fleet anchoring a safe distance from shore, a sloop was sent to contact the locals who had formed a small group waiting on the sandy beach. The mixed group of natives and Portuguese who formed the 'welcome party' made it clear to Dirck Gerritsz – in command of the sloop – that they were not welcome after all and should turn around. The newly-appointed captain hollered back that they were desperate for food and water, having many sick people on board, and that they meant no harm. The locals ultimately gave a 'promise' that they would bring supplies next day for trade. Gerritsz then returned to the fleet to wait, but neither side trusted the other (Barreveld, 2001; 70).

The next day, on the 17th December, the admiral dispatched two pinnaces to the shore. This time the Portuguese waiting there were armed and threatened to fire unless the Dutch returned to their ships immediately. There would be no trade after all. De Cordes then wasted no time in filling all the ships' pinnaces with armed men, being determined to make landfall this time. Captain Bockholt led the attack (Captain Beuningen was still recovering from a serious bout of fever he had contracted in November) and approached with colours flying. They were met with a volley of shots and one of the trumpeters was wounded, but then the locals turned and fled into the forest which fringed the beach. The sick were taken ashore and housed in the now abandoned village (modern-day San Antonio de Palé), with many being put-up in the church. Life was made difficult because the Portuguese continued to snipe at foraging parties from the cover of trees or from the mountainside. At least one man was killed this way, forcing de Cordes to set up a cordon, beyond which his crews were forbidden to go without specific permission. Eventually, on the 24th, he assembled a strong force to clear the whole mountainside. He succeeded, but not without enormous difficulty and further loss of life.

After clearing the mountainside the admiral was able to organize the collection of fresh water for the voyage and seek out stores which had been hidden away by the villagers. A hoard comprising a ton of biscuits, cheese and several barrels of wine was found. Elsewhere cattle were rounded up, and fresh fruit, which was in abundance, was picked from nearby trees (Barreveld, 2001; 72). Everything was rationed out between the crews, and additional preparations were made to continue their journey. The sick were carried back on board, for the problem persisted in these equatorial waters that for every person cured of scurvy another succumbed to fever. The last task was to bury those who had died in these final days, including the English pilot named Thomas Spring who served on the *Hoop*. In total, more than thirty men died at Annobon, and so it was hardly in festive mood that the crews weighed anchor to depart on the 2nd January, 1599. The good news was that, after so long spent on or near this section of African coast, seasonal change should mean the winds were turning in their favour now.

V.   *"... Raine, Winde, Snow, Hayle, Hunger, losses of Anchors, spoyles of Ship and Tackling, Sicknesse, Death, Savages; want of store, and store of wants, conspired a fulnesse of miseries."*[23]

By the time the fleet did embark on the crossing of the Atlantic, Adams was completely recovered from fever and was once again fully functioning as pilot on the *Liefde*. He records with clarity how the fleet struggled at first against the south-easterly trade winds, until: "wee got foure degrees by South the Line; at which time the windes favoured us coming to the South-East, and East South-East, and East" (Purchas, 1625; Bk.3, 125). As the winds veered towards the east, their passage became greatly eased. Adams then goes on to note his main concern: that although some victuals were acquired at Annobon these were still insufficient to sustain the entire fleet for the arduous journey across the South Atlantic.

Admiral de Cordes was also concerned about the level of food supplies, knowing that the next stage of the journey would be much longer than originally planned. After all, the distance from the Guinea Coast of Africa to the shores of South America was more than twice that of the distance from the Cape Verde Islands to the Brazilian coast. He decided to ration the daily allowance of food as soon as they departed Annobon – halving it again to just a quarter-pound of bread per man, with a similar reduction in the quantity of wine and water to be issued. As Adams noted in his letter to Mary:

"scarcitie of Victuals brought such feeblenesse, that our men fell into so great weaknesse and sicknesse for hunger, that they did eate the Calves skinnes, wherewith our Ropes were covered" (Purchas, 1625; Bk.3, 130).

One crew member on board the *Liefde* was so stricken with hunger that he tried to steal bread from the ship's store. A General Council of the captains was called immediately, and the culprit was hung from the bowsprit for all to see before his body was cut-down to fall in the water after nightfall. Adams' concern regarding adequate planning and victualling for a voyage is understandable, given his previous experience as captain of one of the supply ships on the armada campaign, and it is likely that this sort of incident left a lasting impression on him. In later years he did his utmost to ensure crews under his command should not only be well-provisioned but be treated with due regard to all their rights and customs.

To compound the hunger and sickness problems, the range of general duties that the crews had to perform became greater as the condition of the ships deteriorated. Within days of leaving Annobon the main mast of *Het Geloof* broke into pieces, having completely rotted. While the ship was taken under tow by the *Liefde*, all carpenters in the fleet were called to assist in constructing a new mast from the spare spars all ships carried. The repair was good (the ship eventually made the voyage back to Rotterdam), but the effort took-up almost an entire week.

De Weert's account suggests their track took them within sight of Ascension Island, but they carried on rather than attempt a landing. Steering a south-westerly course running parallel to the 'Brasilien' coast, perhaps within the 'smell' of land (at least according to sea-bed evidence from soundings), the admiral was resolute in not making landfall until they reached the Magellan Strait (Barreveld, 2001; 74-75). Off-shore fog-banks were a further sign that the continental shore was near, but the wind turned contrary from time to time and the fleet had to steer away from the coast for fear that they would otherwise be wrecked during the night. Memories of how close the fleet came to disaster on the Guinea coast of Africa still troubled the admiral. Finally, on 29th March land *was* sighted, at a latitude of 50°s according to Adams, and a longitudinal positional fix could be secured. After a crossing of almost three months since leaving Annobon the fleet was safe! In just eight more days, sailing south along the coast, the fleet finally made it to the entrance of the Strait they sought, on 6th April.

With a favourable wind still behind them de Cordes wasted no time entering the Strait so that, after just two more days they had passed the two narrows which guarded the entrance.

Then, on 8th April, where the Strait widened again, an island was spotted full of birds and other wildlife which could only have been Penguin Island (Figure 5). The fleet dropped anchor, and all crews ate well that night. Two days were spent ashore, clubbing penguins – "which are fowles greater than a Ducke" – and filling the cook's stores, and then gathering firewood to cook them. Almost certainly, some of the firewood was used to reduce brine into salt, to cure the penguin meat with so it remained edible for up to two months[24].

Adams felt it was imperative that, having secured sufficient food, anchors should be weighed so that they could continue their passage through the Strait while the wind remained in their favour. The admiral, however, ordered all ships to stay put and the crews to continue collecting more firewood and fresh water. Adams was inwardly furious, and his frustration with this decision remained with him until the days he could vent his fury in both the letter written to his wife in 1605 and to 'Unknown Friends' in 1611. He knew, having probably read accounts of Magellan's voyage through the Strait, and certainly those of Drake and Cavendish, that winter was fast approaching and would bring violent and contrary winds to impede their own passage. Having taken advantage of favourable winds to enter the Strait, they now risked being trapped there for months unless they set sail again immediately.

It had taken Magellan 38 days to complete the passage

having entered the Strait at the beginning of November, in 1520, during the southern hemisphere summer – but the long length of this period was only due to the necessity of exploring many bays and inlets to find the right route. Drake, the second person to successfully navigate the passage, in 1578, had arrived at the entrance too late to avoid contrary seasonal winds, and so had over-wintered on the Atlantic coast where there was better prospect to replenish stores. He entered the Magellan Strait in September, with the onset of summer, and made his way to the Pacific Ocean in just sixteen days. Thomas Cavendish, the third successful explorer, had arrived at the beginning of January – towards the end of the summer season – and as a result battled stormy conditions in the narrow Strait for almost two months before finally emerging from the western exit near the end of February, 1587. As far as Adams and his friend Timothy Shotten (who had served as pilot on the Cavendish expedition, and who was now navigator on the admiral-ship, the *Hoop*) were concerned, enough evidence had been gathered to know that although sudden changes in sea conditions could be anticipated throughout the year, winter was the worst time to be stuck there.

Timothy Shotten would have recalled an incident on the Cavendish expedition which highlighted not just the difficulty of surviving the harsh winters in the Strait, but also the propriety of maintaining progress while the wind was favourable. Shortly after entering the Strait in January, 1587, the attention of Cavendish had been drawn to a small group of Spanish individuals on the northern shore. Sending a boat to investigate, Cavendish came across three men who, they claimed, were the last survivors of an ill-fated attempt by the Spanish crown to establish a small colony in the Strait, in 1584. They were part of a larger group of fifteen men and three women who had decided to abandon their settlement (called San Felipe) and were now trekking overland to try to escape the Strait before the onset of another winter. The original colony of 430 settlers, whose task was to discourage any attempt by other nations to pass through the Strait, had been left with only eight months of supplies and no ship (Burney, 1806; Vol.2, 52). The men Cavendish met had survived three winters without any reprovision. Most of the colony, however, had died from disease, starvation, or attacks from natives, leaving this small remnant who were now desperately in need of aid. Cavendish took one of the three men on board, sending the other two to collect the rest of the group and wait to be picked up. His intention was to take the whole group to Lima, in Peru, and restore them to their fellow countrymen. Cavendish then returned with the boat to his ship, but:

"When the General arrived on board, he found the wind favourable for advancing up the Strait; upon which, without any waiting, he ordered the anchors to be taken up, and the ships immediately sailed forward, leaving the wretched remains of the Spanish colony with this cruel disappointment, added to their other miseries, and utterly abandoned of man, both friend and foe" (Burney, 1806; Vol.2, 69-70).

A few days later, Cavendish came across the abandoned Spanish settlement of San Felipe, a few leagues south of Penguin Island. According to the lone Spanish survivor whom Cavendish had taken on board, the town contained many dead who still lay in their houses, fully clothed (ibid., 73). Nevertheless, the expedition stopped here for five days, taking on fresh water and then "supplied the ships with wood by pulling to pieces the houses in the town" (ibid., 77)[25].

Both Adams and Shotten knew that, between the months of March and September, they could expect to be faced with a cold, prevailing southerly wind, interspersed with a succession of westerly and north-westerly storms and gales and a heavy swell from the west. A winter passage had never been attempted before and, at best, should have been considered both foolhardy and dangerous. Here they were now, well into April, and deep into the Strait, and the admiral was apparently procrastinating over the collection of more firewood while a rare favourable north-easterly wind was blowing. Whatever Adams may have felt about the actions of Cavendish when a favourable wind had suddenly appeared, he knew that if they did not weigh anchor immediately the chance to complete a passage through the Strait might be lost forever.

To his wife Adams wrote:

"...the wind changed, and came Southerly ... All Aprill being out wee had wonderfull much Snow and Ice with great winds. For in April, May, June, July, and August is the Winter there, being in fiftie two degrees $1/2$ by South the Equinoctiall. Many times in the Winter we had the wind good to goe through the Straights, but our Generall (De Cordes) would not." (Purchas, 1625; Bk.3, 130)

The account written to 'Unknown Friends' some years later stated:

"...the Winter came, so that there was much Snow: and our men, through cold on the one side, and hunger on the other, grew weake: wee had the wind at North-East, some five or six days, in which time wee might have passed through the Straights. But, for refreshing of our men, we waited, watering and taking in of wood, and setting up a (large) Pinnace of fifteene or sixteene tunnes in bignesse. At length, wee would have passed through but could not by reason of the Southerly winds, with wet, and also very cold, with abundance of Snow and Ice. Wherefore, we were forced to winter and stay in the Straights from the sixthe of Aprill untill the foure and twentieth of September, in which time the most part of our provision was spent, in so much that for lacke of victuals many of our men dyed through hunger." (Purchas, 1625; Bk.3, 125)

There is a problem with the dates in Adams second letter, but leaving that issue aside for the moment, Adams' rather sketchy narrative of the succession of events encountered during the passage, misses much of the detail contained in de Weert's account. De Weert's version of events suggests Admiral de Cordes *had* tried to keep the fleet moving when winds were favourable (Barreveld, 2001; 79-88). According to de Weert, they could not move from Penguin Island, as desired, because one of the ships in the fleet, the *Het Geloof*, had lost one of her anchors while trying to maintain position in mid-channel. Considerable delay had been caused in trying to retrieve this vital piece of equipment.

In fact, adverse conditions in the Strait caused anchors to be lost with great regularity over the next few weeks. The gale-force gusts of westerly winds, combined with a fast-moving tide due to an unusually large difference between high and low-water marks, made it very difficult for ships to maintain a stable position, especially when no head-way could be made. At times the ships had to resort to deployment of four anchors at once, but the ageing cables and hawsers securing them became frayed and would snap. Making matters worse, the anchor-buoys attached to mark the position of a sunken anchor could also be lost in stormy conditions. Whilst all ships carried reserve anchors, there was a limit to the number of lost anchors that could be replaced. If any ship could not hold position during a storm near land, it was a near certainty that that ship would eventually be wrecked. When, shortly after leaving the Strait, *Het Geloof* lost yet more anchors and cables in a continual succession of storms, Captain de Weert had no choice but to return to Rotterdam, with just one anchor remaining.

The return passage of *Het Geloof* through the Strait offered an opportunity for the pilot, Jan Outghersz, to take further detailed positional plots to construct an accurate chart of these waters – and the way through. Jan Outghersz shared his information with the Dutch map-maker Jodocus Hondius, who published his own version of the chart in 1606 (Wieder, 1924; Vol.2, Appendix *bij*). This chart is shown in Figure 5, where all the places referred to by both de Weert and William Adams are highlighted. This enables a precise understanding of the progress of the Dutch fleet, or lack of it, during that disastrous winter in the Magellan Strait.

The entrance to the Strait lies at $52^1/_2°$s, and the small group of low-lying islets, just beyond the two Narrows, and referred to collectively as Penguin Island, are at $53°$s. Despite shifts in wind the fleet was able to make progress south-west through the first half of the Strait during April, reaching the southernmost point of the passage, known as Cape Froward, at $54°$s. Just before there they had found a good source of freshwater at Mussel Bay which, as the name suggests, also offered a good supply of these shellfish. Then, according to Adams' letter to his wife, having also anchored briefly at nearby Elizabeth Bay they were forced to halt about four leagues (twelve miles) further on by severe winter storms from the west.

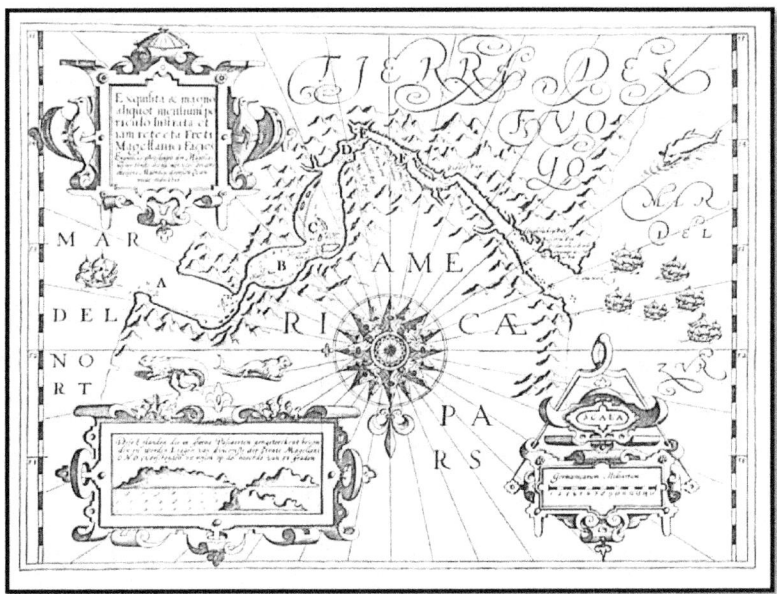

Figure 5. Chart of the Magellan Strait published by Dutch cartographer Jodocus Hondius in 1606 based on the observations of Jan Outghersz, pilot of the Het Geloof.

KEY   **A**: *The entrance to the Strait. Hondius oriented this chart so that south is to the top of the page. The fleet entered the Strait from the left-hand side and exited to the right; as suggested by the group of six ships. The ship exiting to the left is the* Het Geloof, *returning to Rotterdam.*
B: *The short passage between the First and Second 'Narrows'.*
C: *Penguin Island (or Isles).*
D: *Mussel Bay (to the north) and Elizabeth Bay (closest*

> to Cape Froward). *This is also the general area where the Spanish established the town of San Felipe in 1594.*
> **E:** *Cape Froward, the most southerly part of the Strait.*
> **F:** *Cordes Bay, where the fleet spent most of the winter months.*

This leg had taken them beyond Cape Froward to a large inlet they named Cordes Bay, arriving there on 18th April. It was here, ten days later, that Captain Bockholt of the *Trouw* died. After burial on-shore with due ceremony, he was replaced by a young and inexperienced cousin of the admiral, named *Signeur* Balthasar de Cordes. Now that the fleet was on the windward side of the Cape, the enormity of the task ahead became truly apparent. The westerly and wintery storms brought not just bitingly cold winds, with feathered white wave-caps to be struggled against, but also broken ice-flows which could easily damage – if not sink – their frail wooden ships. Indeed, the second of the two small ships they had taken at the Cape Verde islands was lost here in this way, and so it was decided to construct a large pinnace stored in disassembled sections in the hold of the *Hoop*; a task which required eight days. Naming this small ship the *Postillion*, they used it to explore closer inshore when conditions allowed, looking for any source of food and firewood[26].

Sometimes, on these small expeditions, they saw natives, either in canoes or tracking them from the shore. Perhaps because they were half-blinded by snow, or because of tricks played by the pale wintery light in this part of the world, the Dutch estimated them to be exceptionally tall – maybe ten or eleven feet in height (Milton, 2002; 78). The natives were suspicious, and would attack if the opportunity arose, killing some of the crews of shore-parties with their barbed whale-bone tipped harpoons. Equally amazing was the fact that the natives were often completely naked – in such freezing conditions! The Dutch had not adequately prepared for this kind of weather, and felt that their own shirts, jackets, pants, and hose were insufficient to keep out the cold. Admiral de Cordes had to allow the cargo holds to be opened to allow some of the woollen cloth they carried for trade to be fashioned into extra clothing for his men (Barreveld, 2001; 82). Above all, hunger was the main problem and men were dying now on a daily basis. For more than two months the crews were held up here and, as de Weert recorded bitterly – a total of 120 men died for 'want of stores, and a store of wants' in this miserable place (Purchas, 1625; Bk.2, 79).

VI.   "...but in long travels we lost our whole Fleet."[27]

Although the expedition had kept sails on their masts, ready to sail any time the conditions eased sufficiently, it was not until 23rd August that they could eventually depart Cordes Bay (Wieder, 1923; Vol.1, 193)[28]. They had spent more than four long months in this desolate place and it was now the beginning of spring. The weather had slowly begun to improve, but adverse conditions still forced the fleet to anchor from time to time on their way out of Magellan Strait. On one of these occasions de Cordes summoned his captains to remind them of their plans should they become separated in the Southern Ocean, after exiting the Strait.

Sill referring to the 'Atlantic Chart' at this time, the admiral pointed his finger to a sheltered bay on the Chilean coast (at the northern end of the Gulf of Penas). The bay was instantly recognizable on the chart because it lay just to the north of the point where the South American coastline was intersected by the horizontal (east-west) radial line from the nearest compass rose, following latitude 46°15's (Figure 6). This is an important detail, because parallels of latitude were *not* marked so clearly and had to be inferred by navigators using rulers aligned with the single, vertical latitudinal scale in the centre of the chart. The captains agreed to meet in the bay the admiral pointed to, at latitude 46°s, should the need arise.

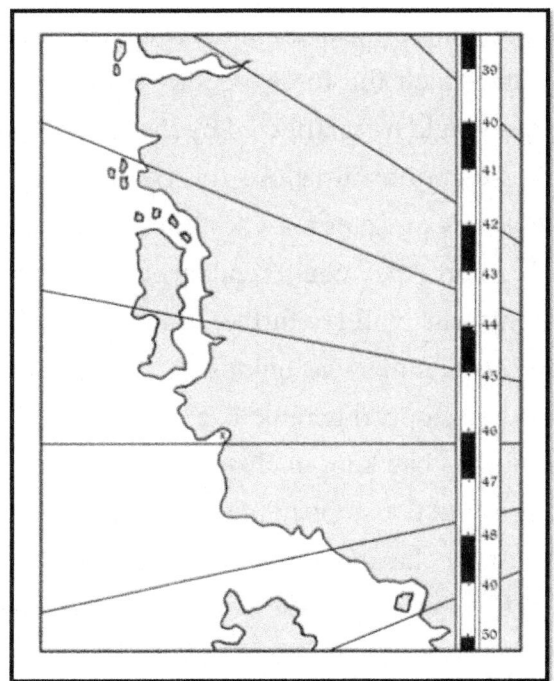

Figure 6. Reconstructed detail from the 'Atlantic Chart' carried on the Liefde *showing the first rendezvous point after leaving the Magellan Strait. Adams stated that this was where the 46° parallel crossed the coast. 'X' marks the spot at the northern shore of the Gulf of Penas where the admiral most likely intended the rendezvous to be. The horizontal line south of the mark is one of the compass-rose radials drawn on the chart and would have helped navigators firmly identify the location. The latitudinal scale was located over the mid-Atlantic on the actual chart, as shown in Figure 1. No other relevant information was shown on the chart in this area.*

This was, in theory, a good plan. Their intent was to raid Spanish assets along the Chilean and Peruvian coasts, and they would need to gather their full force together to ensure success. The Gulf of Penas would be unaffected by the strong Humboldt current which flowed northward along this coast, which would otherwise make it very difficult for a scattered group of ships to assemble. Furthermore, they could rendezvous out of sight of any Spanish settlement, which all lay further to the north. The only known problem was that this was unknown territory, for not even Timothy Shotten had stopped here before. The smaller Drake and Cavendish expeditions had kept in close contact with their respective consorts and not stopped until reaching latitudes 36-$37°_s$, at the Isles of Mocha and Santa Maria, just south of the Spanish colonial town of Concepción on the Chilean coast. Mindful that the rendezvous point was unknown territory, Admiral de Cordes proposed a back-up plan whereby if, after waiting thirty days at the first rendezvous, the fleet remained separated, all ships should proceed to the Isle of Santa Maria and wait there to re-assemble. Unfortunately, there was a far greater and unknown problem with the plan. It was irredeemably flawed because their charts displayed inaccurate latitudinal positions for this section of the coast.

Shortly after this council meeting the fleet's winter woes finally seemed to be over when they sailed through the western approaches to the Strait and the sight of land receded. This was on 3rd September, 1599. In his first letter, Adams reverted to the

Julian calendar and correctly records this date as 24th August (OS) (Purchas, 1625; Bk.3, 130). The Hondius chart (Fig. 5) shows six ships departing the Strait, suggesting that the *Hoop*'s large pinnace, *Postillion*, was still sailing independently of its mother-ship at this point. Some of the smaller pinnaces of the other ships were still being towed when the fleet entered the Southern Ocean, so the fleet slowed to allow for them to be taken back on board. Suddenly, just as a fog-bank began to roll over the ships, the bowsprit of the *Blijde Boodschap* snapped and fell into the sea, threatening to bring the foremast with it. All ships except the *Hoop* saw this, and hove-to in order to offer assistance, including by sending carpenters to the stricken ship (Barreveld, 2005; 91-92). The fog closed-in around them, and the Admiral sailed on, blithely unaware that he was now alone, separated even from his ship's own large pinnace – the *Postillion*.

About a week after the fleet left the Strait, and with the admiral still separated from the other ships, a major storm brewed. Gale force winds battered the ships, veering constantly then sometimes abating. In response, some captains chose to raise sail while others took them down. At one point, during the night of 11th-12th September, the *Liefde* and the now-repaired *Blijde Boodschap* hoisted sail to make better progress, leaving the *Trouw* and *Het Geloof* drifting. Probably, the signal from the Vice-Admiral to set sail had been missed by the two ships left behind. The two pairs of ships never saw each other again and neither, for that matter, was *Postillion* ever encountered again. As the severity of the storm intensified, and as one passing low-pressure system merged into the one ahead, and then the next one following, the whole fleet was forced to the south. Adams recorded reaching latitude 54$\frac{1}{2}$°s, the southernmost point of their entire voyage, noting that it was 'very cold' and, as he no doubt observed quietly, alarmingly close to the bottom edge of his chart.

After a week of continuous storms the weather finally settled. Most of the surviving ships resumed a north to north-westerly course, heading to their pre-determined rendezvous point at 46°s, just off the Chilean coast. The *Hoop,* the *Liefde* and the *Bijlde Boodschap* were now out of sight of each other, as well as the rest of the fleet, whilst the *Trouw* and *Het Geloof* were still sailing in consort (and together made it to an anchorage south of the western entrance to the Magellan Strait)[29]. *Postillion* was lost, almost certainly sunk.

From this point on, the only surviving accounts of the voyage to Japan are found in the two letters Adams wrote. There are discrepancies between the two narratives, particularly regarding dates, but the amount of detail offered is about the same in each. As noted already, the date Adams offers for their departure from the Strait differed by a whole month between the two letters. In the second letter, to Unknown Friends, it could be suggested that he *meant* to write 24th August instead of 24th September, which was the old-style equivalent of the new-style 3rd September found in de Weert's account. The very next two dates mentioned in the letter to his wife, however, are also demonstrably wrong. He records 9th and 29th October as being significant dates but, taken at face value, neither makes any sense in the context of the narrative he goes on to recount. Instead, it would appear he is twice guilty of the same kind of error and should have written September instead of October for both dates. Only with *that* understanding does his story become coherent. Of course, he is almost certainly referring to the Julian calendar in the letter to his wife. These dates are converted to the new style in the present narrative.

So, on 19th September, 1599, the crew of the *Liefde*, now sailing with "a good wind", caught sight of their flagship, the *Hoop*, and "were glad". The two ships sailed in consort for the next "eight or ten days", making good progress towards the rendezvous on the Chilean coast (Purchas, 1625; Bk.3, 130). Then misfortune struck again when another gale overtook them and the *Liefde* lost her fore-sail. Having occurred at night the incident went un-noticed by the crew of the *Hoop*, and the ships parted company again since the *Liefde* could no longer keep up with the admiral ship. The next morning, Adams had no choice but to continue steering for the coast, arriving about ten days later at "the place appointed of our Generall in fortie six degrees", on 9th October; but no other ship was there.

The place where the 46° parallel bisects the Chilean coast is Cape Taitao, which effectively marks the southern boundary of

the Archipelago de Los Chonos. Cape Taitao is a rocky promontory on the northern side of a larger landscape feature called the Taitao Peninsula, the southern flank of which features another headland called Cape Tres Montes (Figure 7). The distance between the two capes is a little over sixty miles and along the southern flank of the peninsula runs the 47° parallel of latitude. This section of coast offers numerous sheltered bays and is, in effect, the northern rim of the
Gulf of Penas. It was at this latitude and in this location that Admiral de Cordes had intended the fleet to reassemble. Stated simply, Adams' intended destination (the rendezvous point) and the point on the coast where his correctly taken astronomical observations had actually taken him differed by almost a whole degree of latitude. The Dutch cartographers who compiled the chart had 'compressed' the coastline here, effectively losing seventy nautical miles. The inevitable outcome was that the ships of the expedition, having lost contact with one another, could not accurately ascertain on their chart where they really were, or effectively locate the rendezvous point. They were all lost, and all had lost sight of each other!

Despite the obvious reality that the *Liefde* had not reached the intended rendezvous point, the priority aboard the ship was to secure food and water, so Captain Beuningen ordered the small pinnace to be lowered to seek a suitable anchorage. They discovered a sheltered bay just south of Cape Taitao where a beach could be accessed easily and soon forage parties were sent out.

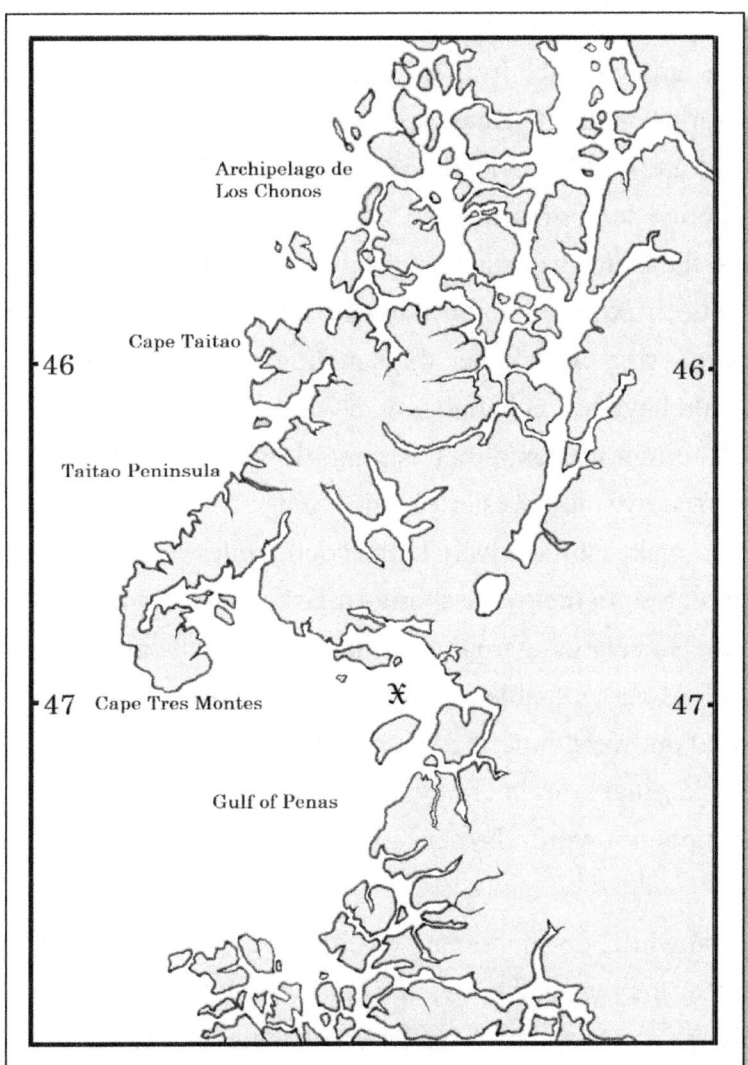

Figure 7. Modern representation of the coast of Chile between latitudes 45°s and 48°s. ✵ *marks the intended rendezvous point of the fleet.*

Once food and watering were arranged, the next task was to assemble the large pinnace from the pieces stored in the hold. This vessel was large enough to carry at least 30 armed men and could sail in open waters, independently of the mother ship. William Adams and other senior mariners in the crew, including his brother Thomas and the Dutch sailing master Jacob van Quaeckernaeck, would have been expected, in turn, to take the pinnace out of the bay to seek any sign of the other ships in the fleet. Sailing the pinnace would have been challenging, however. The off-shore (Humboldt) current was extremely strong, flowing south to north, and was backed by south-westerly trade winds. It was almost impossible to make any headway to the south, unless the pinnace kept position close to the rocky shore – a task that was not just difficult but also very dangerous. Sailing too far to the north created a risk of being unable to return to the *Liefde*. Those men who ventured out were experienced seamen and must have realized quickly that searching beyond the horizon for friendly sails was simply not worth the peril involved.

Meanwhile, on shore, native people were sighted, but it was soon clear they wished to avoid contact "by reason of the Spaniards", as Adams stated in his letter to Unknown Friends. Unbeknown to Captain Beuningen, the indigenous nations were in open conflict with the Spanish, especially to the north where colonial influence had been extended after 1540 following the first Spanish incursions from Peru. Further Spanish progress south, from their new capital at Santiago, had resulted in them founding the township of Valdivia, in 1552, at latitude 40° 50's. A defeat the next year by the original nation, the *Araucanians*, halted further Spanish colonization. An uneasy peace ensued for a few decades until December, 1598, just one year before the arrival here of the *Liefde*, when open war broke out in the region. In fact, at this very point in time, October, 1599, the Araucanians and allied nations were plotting an attack on Valdivia which, on 24th November, resulted in the sacking of the town and a massacre of the inhabitants. These were very tense times indeed.

The native group seen by the foraging parties from the *Liefde* were too far south, and too remote to have been engaged in all this, but they were apparently aware that any contact with European strangers (whom they naturally took to be Spanish) was potentially very dangerous. Captain Beuningen persisted, however, and sent out another party carrying a chest of small items to offer as trade. This time contact *was* established and, in exchange for "Bels and Knives", "they brought us Sheepe and Potatoes" states Adams, "whereof they were very glad". In fact, it was a place where the whole crew could refresh themselves, "finding the people of the Countrey good of nature" (Purchas, 1625; Bk.3, 125). Everyone was extremely surprised, therefore, when after just five or six days "the people went up from their houses into the Countrey, and came no more to us" (ibid.). It was as if the native group had simply melted away. The obvious assumption would be that something had scared or upset the natives, but the reality is that the Taitao Peninsula is an extremely remote place (both then and now) and was sparsely inhabited. The tribesmen were almost certainly semi-nomadic and socially organized in very small groups. It is more likely that they simply did not have the resources for continued trade and, in any case, left according to their annual migratory custom as the height of summer approached. The crew were now left to fend for themselves. Thankfully they found themselves in a highly volcanic, but fertile and forested place where they could fish and forage for food as they waited for the pre-arranged month to pass, hopeful that other ships of the fleet would soon appear.[30]

After four weeks of waiting had passed, or 28 days as Adams notes, the *Liefde* weighed anchor and headed north, the large pinnace sailing alongside. It was 6th November and they made good progress. After just five days of sailing they crossed the 41° parallel and were at the mouth of the river which led to the port and town of Valdivia. Given the political circumstances of the time it was probably just as well that wind and tidal conditions prevented them entering the estuary. The fact Adams mentions Baldivia (Valdivia) at all suggests it was probably the fleets' first intended target for a raid, and Captain Beuningen would certainly have wanted to know if there was any indication the rest of the fleet had been there. It was a moot point, however, because of the state of wind and tide. Beuningen decided to continue sailing with the favourable wind and current to the next designated potential rendezvous, the Isle of Mocha, which they reached the next day.

William Adams was most likely aware that on Drake's voyage of circumnavigation it was at the Isle of Mocha that Francis Drake had been attacked and nearly killed by native people when he went ashore for food and freshwater. The people from the Araucanian nation who lived there had appeared friendly at first and willingly traded food. When Drake returned the next day, however, to collect water with a party of ten unarmed men, they were ambushed by a hundred or more of the local people. The first two sailors ashore were captured and killed, and Drake himself was struck by an arrow in the cheek (Sugden, 2006; 119). This was *Araucanian* nation tribal territory, and the natives in this locale could present themselves as formidable opponents.

The crew of the *Liefde* did not know that the *Araucanian* nation was in open conflict with the Spanish at this time, nor that any attempt to go ashore from these waters was likely to be met with hostile suspicion - or even outright aggression - before any questions were asked. Knowing the previous history of attempts at watering at this island, Adams was probably relieved that none of the other ships in the fleet were waiting here and, since the following wind was too strong to drop anchor anyway, the *Liefde* sailed on to the Isle of Santa Maria, at latitude $37°_s$. The Drake, Cavendish, and other expeditions had all stopped for a while here, and the latitudinal fix was beyond doubt. This time, the *Liefde* charts did not deceive, and a readily recognizable anchorage could be sought. It was also the last of the possible rendezvous points that had been identified by Admiral de Cordes before leaving the

Magellan Strait. Furthermore, the Isle of Santa Maria was located very close to another horizontal line on the chart connecting compass roses, making it somewhat easy to identify.

What followed during the next few days was barely short of disastrous. At this stage the *Liefde* was still - as ever - short of victuals. Captain Beuningen seems to have reasoned that the chances of obtaining sufficient food and water supplies on the mainland were better than getting them on a small island. He therefore ordered the ship to drop anchor en route to the rendezvous point, but within sight of the Isle of Santa Maria. The story is best told in Adams own words; his letters both provide detailed accounts but the following is taken from his second letter, to Unknown Friends:

"…we directed our course for the Island of *Santa Maria*, and the next day we came by the Cape, which is a league and a halfe from the Island, and seeing many people tossed about the Cape, and finding good ground, anchored in fifteene fathom in a faire sandie Bay." (Purchas, 1625; Bk.3, 125-126)

Adams calls this feature the Cape of Santa Maria, but the modern name is Cape Lavapié. It is like a finger of land, pointing directly north to the Isle of Santa Maria. His meaning is not entirely clear, but Adams seems to indicate the ship sailed ("tossed") round the cape, where it formed the headland to a wide bay, looking for a sheltered beach to land. A few miles to the north-east the coast was broken by the estuary of the River Bio-bio, and on its north shore was the Spanish fortified town of Concepción (another possible target for the Mahu expedition). The whole area to the south of the river, including the cape and the islands, was the traditional territory of the *Araucanian* people, and extended as far as Valdavia. Due to the indigenous people's fight for liberation, Spanish colonial hold on the territory of *Araucania* was now extremely tenuous. Adams continues:

"**We went with our boats hard by the water side, to parlee with the people of the land, but they would not suffer us to come a land, shooting great store of Arrowes at our men. Neverthelesse, having no victualls in our Ship, and hoping to find refreshing, wee forcibly landed some seven and twentie or thirtie** (ie. 27-30) **of our men, and drove the wild people from the water side, having most of our men hurt with their Arrowes. They being onland, we made signes of friendship, and in the end came to parlee with signes and tokens of friendship, which the people understood. So, wee made signes, that our desire was to have victualls for Iron, Silver and Cloth, which we shewed them. Wherefore they gave our folke Wine, with Batatas to eate, and other fruits, and bid our men by signes and tokens to goe aboord, and the next day to come againe, and then they would bring us victualls: so, being late our men came aboord, the most part of them being hurt more or lesse, and yet we were very glad that we had come to a parlee with them, hoping that we should get refreshing.**" (ibid.)

Despite their wounds (in the letter to his wife, Adams states only eight or nine men had been injured) the crew had received a meal and wine, and the general mood was a happy one. After all, a clear promise had been made for substantial supplies to be delivered the next day. Some of the crew had doubts, however; they recalled the story of Drake's adventures in this very same area (the Isle of Mocha), at almost the same time of year. Drake had received a friendly reception on first landing, and received similar promises, but he and his crew were nearly massacred the following day when they returned. The sceptics would have been reminded, on the other hand, how they never had trouble with the native group they had met a few weeks ago at Cape Taitao. Whatever, the arguments and banter would be resolved at a general meeting to be called first thing the following morning.

The meeting is not referred to in the letter to Adams' wife, but his account there does give a much clearer and accurate idea of when exactly this all occurred, albeit using the old-style calendar. In the new-style, this day dawned as Saturday, 13th November (Purchas, 1625; Bk.3, 130). The letter to Unknown Friends suggests otherwise, but continues the narrative nevertheless:

"The next day, being the ninth of November, 1599, our Captaine, with all our Officers prepared to goe a land, having taken counsell to goe to the waterside, but not to land more than two or three men: for there were people in abundance,

and were also unknowne; our men therefore were willed not to trust them. This counsell being concluded, the Captaine himselfe went in one of our Boats, with all the force that we had: and being by the shore side, the people of the countrie made signes that they should come a land; but that did not like our Captaine well." (Purchas, 1625; Bk.3, 126)

It seems Captain Beuningen, 'the general', was keen to take all the able-bodied men available, despite the general meeting's conclusion that absolute discretion had to be employed and only a few men should be deployed on shore to minimize the potential risk to all. Even so, there were fewer men than had gone ashore the previous day, almost certainly reflecting the severity of some of the wounds received then. It also seems likely that the captain felt it was his duty to lead the men this time, having watched events from the ship the day before.

"In the end the people comming not neere unto our Boats, our Captaine, with the rest resolved to land, against that which was concluded in our Ship, before the going on land. At length three and twentie men landed with Muskets, and marched up towards foure or five houses, and when they were about a Musket-shot from the Boates, more than a thousand Indians who lay intrenched, immediately fell upon our men with such weapons as they had, and killed them all to our knowledge." (ibid.)

In the letter to his wife, Adams offers a slightly different version of events:

> "**The next day our Captaine, and three and twentie of our chiefe men went on land, meaning for marchandize to get victuals, having wonderfull hunger. Two or three of the people came straight to our Boat in friendly manner, with a kind of Wine and Rootes, with making tokens to come on land, making signes that there were Sheep and Oxen. Our Captaine with our men, having great desire to get refreshing for our men, went on land. The people of the Countrey lay intrenched a thousand and above, and straight-way fell upon our men, and slew them all; among which was my brother *Thomas Adams*. By this losse we had scarse so many men whole, as could weigh our Anchor.**" (Purchas, 1625; Bk.3, 130)

Only the handful of men who had been left behind to keep watch in the two pinnaces survived. Stunned, they waited and waited for any of their friends to show signs of life and come back, but in vain. Very reluctantly, as the sun went down, they turned back towards the *Liefde* with their "sorrowfull newes".

On board the *Liefde* the mood was grim. The two most senior officers on board now were the master, or *schipper*, Jacob van Quaeckernaeck, and navigator William Adams. Naturally, Quaeckernaeck would assume the role of captain, since Beuningen is likely to have given such verbal instruction before setting off.

All grieved the sudden loss of so many mess-mates, and Adams particularly mourned for his younger brother (although he gives no indication of his feeling in his letter). They stayed at anchor for that night, and next morning, then, after checking once more for signs of any survivors they set course for the Isle of Santa Maria, just a few miles away. They were all still hungry, of course, but their spirits were greatly lifted when they sighted the flagship *Hoop* directly in front of them, already at anchor in the 'roads' of the island. Both crews were overjoyed to re-unite after being separated for six weeks. But the admiral was not there to greet the *Liefde*, and expressions of joy belied feelings of true grief shared on both ships. A sense of disbelief quickly permeated both crews as they realized they had both suffered very similar losses. Simon de Cordes together with a total of twenty-seven officers and crew of the *Hoop* had been murdered by native people on the Isle of Mocha in almost the same circumstances as Beuningen and his men at Cape Lavapié.

In just a few short days the two ships had lost half their crews, and both captains – the admiral and vice-admiral - were dead too. The Mahu expedition was now facing complete failure.

VII. *"So against their wils they made composition with us, which within the time appointed they did accomplish."*³¹

The *Hoop* had been at the Isle of Santa Maria for four days, having departed the Isle of Mocha on 10ᵗʰ November, the day before the *Liefde* arrived there. It was clear that the rendezvous point *they* had sought on the coast in October had been close to the *Liefde*'s position. Unbeknown to either crew the *Blijde Boodschap* had been in that general vicinity too, and now was very close to their present position at the Isle of Santa Maria. Dates are unclear but, possibly that night, or the night before (13-14ᵗʰ November), the ship sailed past the island, carried along by the combination of strong wind and current. With a crew of only nine able-bodied men now, Captain Dirck Gerritsz was unable to turn about, and so made the fateful decision to continue sailing north and head for the Spanish port of Valparaiso, not far from the regional capital of Santiago. He arrived there on 17ᵗʰ November and surrendered his ship and crew to the Spanish authorities (Barreveld, 2001; 127-129)³².

Even before that event the Spanish knew of the presence of both the *Hoop* and the *Liefde* at the Isle of Santa Maria. In fact, this was the most urgent concern facing the crews now. Just an hour or so before the *Liefde* arrived at the anchorage the officers on the flagship had welcomed aboard a Spanish official sent from the town of Concepción. He had been dealt with politely and then ushered away as quickly as possible, but only on the promise he could return the next day, the 15th November. The officers on the *Hoop* had pleaded their peaceful intent, but it was far from clear that the Spanish visitor had been convinced. It was now vital that a plan should be drawn-up for how to deal with a return visit the next day or, worse, an armed enemy warship appearing round the headland.

Luckily (but unbeknown to the Dutch), the Spanish fleet in the Pacific was deployed on the Peruvian coast and was no immediate threat. The Spanish governor in Chile, who was subordinate to the viceroy in Lima, normally resided in Santiago, but earlier in the year had come south to be close to the frontier towns of Valdivia and Nueva Imperial because of the unrest in this territory. At this moment, Governor Fransisco Quiñones was in Concepción, less than twenty-five miles away from the Dutch. Responding to an urgent request from the inhabitants of Nueva Imperial for emergency supplies ahead of a likely siege he had sent a small fleet with food provisions on the 11th or 12th November.

Making only slow headway against the southerly breeze, the boats, under the command of Captain Pedro de Recalde, pulled into the leeward shore of the Isle of Santa Maria. Separated only by a narrow headland from the *Hoop*, Recalde spotted the masthead and lookout of what he assumed to be an English pirate. He immediately dispatched one of his boats back to Concepción to inform the governor, before later continuing his mission to the south. Governor Quiñones responded by sending an emissary, Captain Antonio Recio, in one of the few boats now available to him, first to arm the few Spanish colonists on the island, and then to approach the ship to find out more (IJzerman, 1915; 49). It seems he confronted the new captain of the *Hoop* about midday on the 14th November and was invited to come aboard.

The ship's lookout had been sharp enough to have seen Recalde two days earlier, which gave the crew time to prepare for a formal visit by the Spanish colonial authorities. Thus began an amazing act of deception, into the middle of which had sailed the *Liefde*, totally unwittingly. The expected visit duly came, but the crew of the *Hoop* ensured it did not last any longer than necessary and that the Spanish emissary had no time for a good look around. Once Captain Recio had boarded, formalities were exchanged and the declaration made that the *Hoop* was a peaceful Dutch trading vessel with no other intent but to buy and sell merchandise. With a touch of bravado Recio was assured that the Dutch were quite well-provisioned but would be happy to take on any more victuals that might be traded. He had no need to be reminded, of course, that the Dutch were faithful subjects of the Spanish since the Netherlands were, after all, a Spanish possession. Recio regretted that a trade permit would be required first, and that he would have to return to Concepción to report back and obtain one. Formalities completed, he departed, promising to return as soon as he could.

It must have been with an element of nervous exhaustion, tinged with the mixed emotions of grief and joy, that the crew of the *Hoop* had watched the approach of the *Liefde* and her pinnaces on that Sunday. Unfortunately, the arrival was also observed by Captain Recio, and sight of the equally well-armed ship merely furthered his growing conviction that he was dealing with brigands.

That evening, the surviving officers and merchants on the Dutch ships had to get their heads together to determine their next course of action. Above all, they were desperate for food and drink and realized that since, for obvious reasons, they could not rely on the native population to re-supply them they would have to turn to the Spanish for help. To do this, however, they had to maintain a show of strength, otherwise the Spanish would seize them with ease. Already, it seems, the crew of the *Hoop* had tried to do this, not only by gathering as many fit men as they had on deck, all displaying an air of nonchalance, but also by offering the fiction that the admiral Simon de Cordes, was very much alive and well. No mention at all had been made of the disastrous events of a few days ago, just as if – in fact – they never happened. This deceit has led to one of the great mysteries of the Mahu expedition. Exactly *who* was now in command of the *Hoop* now that de Cordes was dead? Who had received the Spanish emissary on the quarterdeck, under the guise of captain of the Dutch vessel (or, after the unexpected arrival of the *Liefde*, admiral of the fleet)?

The Spanish envoy, Recio, was evidently convinced that he had indeed met the Dutch leader, even if he was unconvinced by their display of *braggadocio*. He later wrote in his report to the governor that he had been received by Admiral Simon de Cordes, but was amazed at his youthful age, which he estimated to be 19 or 20 years old (IJzerman, 1915; 51). The Dutch, perceiving his obvious surprise when he first met the 'admiral', had quickly explained that he was the *son* of the late Simon De Cordes, also named Simon, or Simon de Cordes Junior (even though no such man had taken part in the voyage). Unfortunately, they interposed, his father had passed away earlier in the voyage and had named the younger Simon as his successor. There was no reason to disbelieve the lie, especially when, much later, it was learnt (from the captured crew of the *Blijde Boodschap*) that Simon de Cordes Senior had been in his early forties, having spent much of his life living in Portugal where he had married. Recio was not a complete fool, however, and realized that something strange was going on. He very much doubted the stated motives of the Dutch.

The Dutch themselves must have been very aware of the pantomime nature of their ruse – but felt they had to persevere with the charade. At their enforced Council meeting on the night of the 14th November they decided that, first, some of the crew of the *Liefde* would be transferred to the *Hoop* to make it appear the vessel was fully-manned. Then, everything was to be made shipshape, and the pick of the merchandise taken out of the hold to show the envoy, and to offer as a possible trade. The best surviving bottles of wine would be brought out to entertain their Spanish guest. Also, they were going to sit down together, straight away, to compose a letter, in Spanish, to send to Governor Quiñones to reinforce the notion that they were, indeed, trusted allies of Spain.

A copy of this letter was found by the Chilean historian Crescente Errazuriz in 1881. Described as being very much a Spanish chauvinist (IJzerman, 1915; 4), he wrote:

"…in the incomprehensible copy of the letter which … the Hollanders addressed to the Governor of Chile, and that I have before me, I see that among the commanders of the fleet, which they maintain is a mercantile fleet, they seem to describe Simon de Cordes as 'the father of our general'" (cited in IJzerman, 1915; 51, translated from Dutch by the author).

In a rather bizarre twist, this quote has been taken by subsequent scholars as convincing evidence that Recio had been correct in believing that the new admiral was indeed Simon de Cordes Junior (ibid.). But, of course, the Dutch were obliged to perpetuate the farcical lie in their letter. For one thing, if the fictitious younger Simon had been born and brought up in Portugal, the letter should have made far more sense than Errazuriz could make of it. Judging by his account the letter had been written by mariners or merchants with only a passing knowledge of Portuguese and/or Spanish. William Adams was such a man; he could converse in

Spanish[33] but would be hard pushed to write a formal letter in that language, just like most of his surviving friends and fellow officers. In fact, it is Adams' account in his letter to his wife that has helped solve the mystery, for he claims the "new admiral" was "a young man, one *Hudcopee*" (Purchas, 1625; Bk. 3, 131).

Credence must be given to this part of his letter, for Adams had no reason in 1605 (when he wrote it) to attempt to deceive anyone in this matter. After all, he had just described a huge catastrophe to befall the Dutch. The name may seem unusual but was actually a fairly common Dutch surname: Huijdecoper, or Huydecoper. It does not occur anywhere else in accounts of the expedition, but nor for that matter does Simon de Cordes Junior, or the names of many other seamen still unknown. One famous individual of that name, however, is Jacob Jansz Huydecoper who was a captain on Olivier van Noort's successful expedition which also departed Rotterdam in 1598, shortly after Mahu's expedition had left. It has been suggested that Adams confused this individual with someone else when he wrote "Hudcopee", but this is unlikely since he is talking of his admiral, whom he would have known well. Also, Jacob Jansz was known to have served as midshipman on the first Dutch East Indies expedition of 1595, and so should hardly be described as "a young man" by Adams. The rest of Adams' description is also hardly appropriate, for Hudcopee "…knew nothing, but had served the Admirall" (ibid.).

The clear implication is that Hudcopee was no mariner; he

was merely someone who had been Simon de Cordes' favourite; a young gentleman companion. Perhaps he was nominated by Simon de Cordes to be his successor, but this would have been based entirely on the young man's potential wealth and social status, as well as his affection. It was certainly not based on his skills of seamanship, or ability to command. But Adams at least would have already learned, from his experience in the Queen's navy, that the qualification for captaincy was not always an ability to set sails or steer a course; rather it could be simply money and influence. After the surprise death of Admiral de Cordes on the Isle of Mocha, and other senior officers as well, the surviving crew would not have had time to fully reorganize before the arrival of the Spanish emissary. Faced with the knowledge that the Spanish would arrive soon the crew had persuaded young Hudcopee to assume the role of admiral and the name of de Cordes. They were in dire straits anyway and, at worst, he might act as scapegoat. He was probably an unpopular crewmate anyway, given his favour with the real de Cordes despite his inabilities at sea. Now, the combined crews of two ships relied on him to carry on the deception. Hudcopee would have to put on the admiral's hat, cape, and sword again the next day to continue acting as if he was Simon de Cordes' son - and be convincing.

In Adams' words, in the same letter to his wife: "And so the next day he (the Spaniard) came againe, and we let him depart quietly". It was probably with great relief that they waved him off, for the deception *seemed* still to be working. Given the distance between Concepción and the Isle of Santa Maria, it almost certainly took at least 24 hours for Recio to return and consult with the governor, and then sail back for his second visit. It was probably late afternoon when he had returned to the ship, therefore, and he was invited to spend the night on board, though this offer was politely refused. He would have been asked to join them for dinner, however, - a meagre affair for certain - and given a tour of the ship. He was thus denied any opportunity to visit the *Liefde* before nightfall. Although all interaction was polite, he was keeping an eye on all things and assessing everything keenly. As he took the letter written the previous night from the 'admiral' and prepared to depart he knew that something, probably many things, were not right. He had counted the crew to be just 47 or 48 men but feared that the *Hoop* was still well-capable of firing a broadside or two. His impression was that the *Liefde* was not in such a good state, and that despite assurances otherwise, the ships were very low on supplies. Feigning friendship, he suggested to Hudcopee that if he brought his ships into the harbour at Concepcíon, all the supplies the Dutch needed would be made available (Wieder, 1923; Vol.1, 314-315).

The Spaniard's intent was to bring about the capture of the Dutch ships without any exchange of gunfire. Both ships could be taken when they came peacefully to port in Spanish territory, by overpowering the crews as soon as they came to anchor. The Dutch, of course, were highly suspicious and would not allow the ruse to work – but how else could victuals be obtained? All they could do was watch and wait for an opportunity to arise. According to Adams, that opportunity came the very next day, when:

"…came two Spaniards aboard us without pawne (agreement), **to see if they could betray us. When they had seene our Shippe, they would have gone on land againe; but we would not let them, shewing that they came without leave; whereat they were greatly offended. We shewed them that we had extreame neede of Victualls, and that if they would give us so many Sheepe, and so many Beeves, they should goe on land. So against their wils they made composition with us, which within the time appointed they did accomplish."** (Purchas, 1625; Bk.3, 130-131)

It is not easy to know who these Spaniards were, or what had been their precise intention. Spanish records make no mention of the incident, but this is hardly surprising, and it is certain that both the *Hoop* and *Liefde* were re-supplied before attempting to cross the Pacific. Unfortunately, Adams second letter does not elaborate, simply noting that "…having refreshed ourselves in the Island *Santa Maria*, more by policie than by force…" they were ready to depart.

One of the unlucky 'intruders' on the *Hoop* was perhaps a pilot, prepared to take the vessel into Concepción. Certainly the two men were both considered important enough to force the hand of Governor Quiñones. The Spanish fleet could not be called upon since they were too far away to give immediate assistance. And Adams gave a very precise (and accurate) measurement for the Dutch location in his second letter, at 37°12`s, confirming they were still at anchor in the roads of Santa Maria, where land forces could not approach them either. The date of the kidnap of the two Spanish officials was probably 17th November, and the Governor of Chile was preoccupied with the native uprising which was reaching a frightening climax. He was, perhaps, prepared to starve out the Dutch at first, not just to allow time to sort out a face-saving solution, but also to concentrate on more pressing issues. Then, on 24th November, came the shocking news that the important town of Valdivia had fallen to the *Araucanian* nation. It was the beginning of 'the destruction of seven cities' and led very quickly to the loss of Spanish control of all territory south of Concepción and the River Bio-bio[34]. The governor could no longer afford not just the distraction but also the potential threat of Dutch intervention. Over the next two days the *Hoop* and the *Liefde* were revictualled with all the food and drink they required, on the promise that they release the two hostages and depart the shores of Chile immediately.

VIII. "... it was resolved to go for Japon"[35]

While waiting for a resolution of the crisis at Santa Maria, a Council was held aboard the flagship *Hoop* involving both captains and the surviving pilots of each ship. On the assumption that the problem of victualling would be resolved, consideration had to be given to the next course of action or, specifically, the course to be sailed. The decision to head for Japan was not unexpected. That destination was almost certainly named in the original orders for the expedition and was the reason why Dirck Gerritsz had been invited to join the voyage. Well-known to Van Linschoten, whom he had met in Goa, Dirck (or 'Pomp') Gerritsz was the only known Dutchman to have ever visited Japan, having served as gunner on a Portuguese merchantman which made the voyage there in 1585. He was not actually present at this meeting, having been made captain of the *Blijde Boodschap* (one of the missing ships). His advice, however, that woollen broadcloth would find a better market in the cooler climes of Japan than in the hot, tropical spice islands known as the Moluccas, was still familiar to those present.

The fact that broadcloth formed the main trade item in the holds of the *Hoop* and the *Liefde* clearly influenced the decision to continue the plan to head for Japan, even without Gerritsz. It was also the reason why, perhaps, the decision was taken to continue the voyage with two ships, both with depleted crews, rather than scuttle one of the vessels and combine the crews on a single ship. The latter option would have resulted in the loss of up to half of the most valuable trade items they carried – and a subsequent loss of potential profit.

The most influential voice during the meeting was almost certainly that of Timothy Shotten, pilot of the *Hoop*. He was the only person in the expedition with actual experience of crossing the Pacific Ocean, having sailed in the 1586-88 voyage of Thomas Cavendish to complete only the third ever circumnavigation of the world. He would have had painful memories of the decision taken by Cavendish to scuttle one of his ships because of a crew shortage before the Pacific crossing. The result was a lack of space to carry all the valuables they subsequently captured from the Spanish treasure ship *Santa Ana*; said to have been "one of the richest vessels that ever sailed on the seas". The treasure that could not be taken had to be sunk along with the Spanish vessel off the shores of modern southern California (Wilson, 2003; 53). If Shotten had any say in the decision whether to continue this voyage in one or two ships he probably voted to keep both ships; even if under-crewed. He would not have wished to lose a substantial share of any profit generated for a second time in his life! As Adams also notes, rather dryly, neither captain of the two ships wished to give-up their newly-appointed commands anyway (Purchas, 1625; Bk.3, 126). Indeed, the flotilla that would soon set sail consisted of three ships if the large pinnace from the *Liefde* was included, which could be crewed by less than ten seamen and would offer even more storage space.

One issue which was now very clear was that there was no longer any possibility of emulating the exploits of Drake and Cavendish. With the fleet now reduced to only two principal ships, with no sight or knowledge of the whereabouts of the other three, the ships had to depart as soon as they were re-victualled. Their presence off Chile was known to the Spanish, as well as the fact there were insufficient men for them to both sail the ship *and* fight, however well-armed. The element of surprise was completely lost, and to contemplate sailing further up the coast for raiding and pirating, as both Drake and Cavendish had done, was now completely out of the question. The decision was made to 'go for Japan', but which route should they take; the journey had never been attempted before? Compounding the problem, the charts they had been issued with did not span the whole of the Pacific Ocean and could not provide any clear indication of the bearing they should take when departing the Chilean coast.

Adams and Shotten would have to turn to the globes that they (or at least Adams) had carried on board as part of their personal possessions. Their compatriot John Davis, who was engaged as pilot on one of the other Dutch expeditions which departed in 1598, had described in his book *The Seamans' Secrets* how to obtain the correct bearing for navigation using just a terrestrial globe. The globe made by Molyneaux in Adams' locker, and possibly a world chart showing the same content displayed on the Mercator projection, printed by the Dutch cartographer Hondius, highlighted the routes taken by Drake and Cavendish during their circumnavigations[36]. Using all this information Adams and Shotten, in conjunction with their respective captains, could plot a great-circle route connecting their present location at the Isle of Santa Maria to the southernmost cape of Japan. Such a route would resemble a 'reverse S-shape' on a flat chart, taking them first in a westerly direction, then veering northerly to cross the equator, then westerly again to reach Japan. Such a route sounds complicated but represents the shortest distance between setting off and reaching their destination; a journey of almost exactly 11,000 miles.

A modern-day airline pilot would certainly follow the great-circle route, but to Timothy Shotten, an experienced sea-captain, such a course was counter-intuitive. On the Cavendish expedition they had first made good progress south of the equator by following the South American coast with the help of the Humboldt Current. North of the equator, however, sailing up the North American coast, they had encountered a contrary current. Later, they made the fastest yet crossing of the Pacific, beating Drake's time from Baja California to the Mariana Islands by three weeks, the whole crossing taking just forty-five days (Wilson, op. cit.). Shotten reckoned, therefore, that they should defer the westward stage of their voyage until they reached the equator, or perhaps just north of it between the latitudes of 13^0N and 16^0N, where he had already made one successful crossing. Then, as they knew from reports of the Portuguese trade with China and Japan, progress north along the Asian coastline would also be met with a favourable ocean current. In other words, Shotten proposed an alternative S-shaped route, tracking northerly first, then west, and then northerly again.

Perhaps Shotten also argued that this course would maximise the use they could make of the charts they *did* have, using the globe to track their westward progress along a course that he, at least, had already sailed once. On reaching the North Mariana Island chain, shown on their chart by Doedsz as the *Islas de las Velas*, they could follow a north-north-westerly bearing to 'island-hop' to the supposed southern cape of Japan. Adams, Quaeckernaeck, and certainly Hudcopee, were in no position to disagree, and so this became the accepted plan. Then, when the Spanish relented and re-supplied the ships, the *Hoop* and the *Liefde*, together with the large pinnace, were finally able to depart the roads of the Isle of Santa Maria on 27th November, 1599. They left, of course, with a somewhat heavy heart, for they had still not seen any of the other ships of the Mahu fleet.

Whether or not Hudcopee maintained effective control of the flotilla as they left the Chilean coast simply cannot be known, since Adams never mentions him again. The master of the *Hoop*, Cornelius Jansz, had been murdered alongside Simon de Cordes by natives, and the 'under skipper' had been on the *Postillion*. Timothy Shotten was the only surviving senior officer in charge of sailing matters and would certainly have guided the ships into these uncharted waters. He wished to be out of sight from land, of course, for fear that they would be chased by the Spanish. If they sailed too far to the west, however, they would begin to lose the beneficial influence of the Humboldt Current. Luckily, the route they had planned kept them in a zone which benefited from both the strong current and the ever-reliable south-easterly trade winds, especially after passing 30°s.

From about 20°s the *Hoop* and the *Liefde*, with the large pinnace still sailing in consort, began to pick up the influence of the South Equatorial Current, encouraging them to assume a more westerly direction. All went very well, and in the letter to his wife Adams described how the two ships, constantly in sight of one another, 'passed the line Equinoctiall with a faire wind, which continued good for diverse monthes.' Given their experience south of the Cape Verde Islands the year before, when a combination of contrary winds and currents meant they could not progress further west, they would not have been too surprised when they suddenly encountered similar conditions in the low latitudes north of the equator. They were crossing the Equatorial Counter Current, which slowed them, but did not halt their progress. Then, after reaching about 10°N, they met the North Equatorial Current which bore them westward once more. They had reached the route sailed by Cavendish, as well as Drake and Magellan before him.

Adams continues the narrative in the letter to his wife:

"In our way we fell with certain Islands in sixeteene degrees of North-latitude, the Inhabitants whereof are men-eaters. Comming neere these Islands, and having a great Pinnesse with us, eight of our men beeing in the Pinnesse, ranne from us in the Pinnesse, and (as we suppose) were eaten of the wild men, of which people we tooke one: which afterward the Generall sent for to come into his Shippe." (Purchas, 1625; Bk.3, 131)

The sighting of the Mariana islands marked an important way-point on the journey[37]. All three of the circumnavigators to date; Magellan, Drake, and Cavendish, had stopped here (on one or other of the islands) to mark the end of their Pacific crossing and the opportunity to replenish supplies. Fresh water was required and was in abundant supply on some of these ancient volcanic mountainsides. The archipelago included the well-known names (today) of Guam, Tinian, and Saipan, but Adams' account suggests it was just to the north of these that the *Hoop* and the *Liefde* made first sighting of the islands and islets. The indigenous population, known as the *Chamorro* nation, were excellent seafarers and raced out to meet/greet, or perhaps turn-away, any great ship they saw approaching from the east. All previous explorers had encountered the same vista – of fast lateen-sailed dug-out boats with out-riggers approaching them, filled with warrior-like young males paddling furiously. Enemy or friends? Bellicose or welcoming? Men-eaters or just curious folk?

Magellan found these people a nuisance. As with all expeditions of this era at least one pinnace was carried on each ship which would be lowered away from the main deck to carry out ship-to-ship or ship-to-shore transfers of men and stores. If used regularly, as was likely after land had been sighted, it would be towed behind the ship. Although the native people offered gifts, they felt free to pilfer goods they valued (particularly metals), but Magellan's patience was broken when his pinnace was stolen. He retrieved it by resorting to force, shooting the offenders, and setting alight the nearest village. He also dubbed the islands (around Guam) *Islas de los Ladrones* – the 'Isles of Thieves'. Others called the area *Islas de las Velas Latinas*, or the 'Isles of Lateen Sails', which became shortened on Doedsz' map to *Islas de las Velas* or, simply, the 'Isles of Sails'. Drake encountered similar problems and resorted to a shoot to kill policy to frighten-off "thieving savages", killing at least twenty (Wilson, 2003; 42). When the *Hoop*, the *Liefde* and the "great Pinesse" arrived, the same scene confronted the crews. There is no evidence whatsoever that the native *Chamorro* were man eaters, as Adams suggested. Perhaps this was simply a rumour promulgated by the Spanish to deter other ships from re-victualling there. Certainly, both crews were very wary, however, given their terrible experience with the indigenous people of Chile.

William Adams' description, which is the only known

account of the events here, does not give any indication of how long the voyage to this point had taken. But the crews of all three ships must have required fresh water as well as food supplies, and so they needed to make landfall. The story he recounts, therefore, does not quite ring true. Why would eight crew members who were sailing the pinnace attempt to desert the flotilla *before* any landing had been either attempted or achieved? The ship they were in consort with, the *Liefde*, still had one small pinnace which could follow them to shore and effect a capture and inflict punishment. So too, as far as is known, did the *Hoop*.

Both the *Hoop* and the *Liefde* were still very well-armed, and an alert landing party should have been able to fend for itself, at least on first encounter with the native population. The *Chamorro* people too would be extremely wary of the potential danger of firearms being used against them, as local oral traditions of previous encounters with great ships from the east would have emphasized that risk. Timothy Shotten seemed *not* to harbour any bad memories of the islanders and would not have recommended the *Islas de las Velas* as a waypoint if he had any negative views about replenishing supplies here. It would seem likely, therefore, that all three vessels dropped anchor at this tropical paradise and sent shore parties to greet the local people, trading some of the smaller items such as knives and bells which they carried in abundance as a sign of friendship and for seeking permission to re-victual.

It is impossible to know the precise location of the expedition's landing; indeed, it might even have been on one of the larger isles, such as Guam, where both Magellan and Cavendish had first sighted the islands. Guam lies in the latitude of $13^0{}_N$ – $14^0{}_N$, and Saipan is around $15^0{}_N$. In fact, the North Mariana Islands extend from Guam to about $21^0{}_N$, but Doedsz' chart, used by Shotten and Adams, suggests the island chain only extended north as far as $16^0{}_N$. This was the latitude at which Adams states the desertion of eight crew took place. As far as Adams knew it was at this latitude that the *Islas de las Velas* would be left behind, and the final leg of the voyage to Japan would begin. It seems likely, then, that the theft of the pinnace took place as the ships were leaving the islands, rather than before they attempted to set foot on land.

Under such a scenario it is possible to envisage that after the flotilla first sighted the *Islas de las Velas*, with the large pinnace of the Liefde still sailing in consort, they made a relatively peaceful landing on one of the islands in the chain. They probably spent a few days ensuring full replenishment of victuals. Some thieving may have taken place, but in return the crew of the *Liefde* were able to negotiate the services of a local pilot (a common practice at that time). Leaving the islands, in a scene perhaps foretelling the mutiny on the *Bounty*, and probably under the cover of nightfall, the eight crew of the pinnace turned their vessel around and returned to the island where they had been made welcome. By the time the theft was realized it was already too late to make chase or seek retribution. But why should Adams have felt inclined to mislead his wife regarding this, in his otherwise very detailed account of the voyage?

The answer lies, perhaps, in the context in which the letter to his wife was sent. Written in 1605, it was entrusted to the captain of the *Liefde*, Jacob Quaeckernaeck, and another friend and shipmate, Melchior Saantvort, to carry back to England when they eventually left Japan[38]. Adams knew the Dutch would read the letter (indeed they seem to have deliberately 'lost' the last few pages) and he did not wish to write anything that would impugn the character of his friends. The desertion, perhaps even mutiny, of a significant number of the crew of the *Liefde* would surely reflect badly on the captain and, possibly writing in collusion with Quaeckernaeck, Adams wished to record the event in the best possible light. The need to have even mentioned it at all was probably occasioned by the fact that news of such deeds could spread surprisingly quickly. The next 'great ship' to have visited the islands would surely have heard another version of the story, and Adams wished to ensure his account was also in circulation to counter any claims of potential mis-management on board the *Liefde*. He implied the rest of the flotilla did not attempt to stop at the islands because they were fearful of cannibalism. This is, of course nonsense, as Shotten would have known. But, if this *is* the reason for Adams' account, the story of the *Chamorros* being eaters of men is more likely to have been an Anglo-Dutch invention than a Spanish one.

The next, and supposedly final stage of the voyage proved to be not only difficult but almost disastrous. By the 22nd February, 1600, the two ships had reached the latitude of $28^0{}_N$, about half-way between the Tropic of Cancer and the southern-most part of mainland Japan. After just under ninety days crossing the Pacific Ocean from Chile to Japan ... they were almost there! But then they encountered a squall which turned into a full-blown storm: "...a wonderfull storme of wind, as ever I was in, with much raine..." (Purchas, 1625; Bk.3, 126). After three days of unrelenting bad weather, being tossed about by mountainous waves, Adams records that they parted from their companion ship: "The foure and twentieth of February we lost sight of our Admirall, which afterward we saw no more" (Purchas, 1625; Bk.3, 131).

With no indication of longitude it is not easy to say exactly where this storm was encountered. At this time of year, near the height of Japan's winter monsoon period when a northerly wind with origins in Siberia prevails, it was certainly not a tropical storm – or typhoon. Although typhoons have been recorded at all times of year in Japanese waters, the season for them is generally late-summer, from August through October. Rather, this was likely to be an intense, blustery, wintery storm which typically track along a well-defined seasonal weather front just to the south of Japan. Since the front typically meanders to the north, near Hokkaido, after passing to the east of the mainland, storms which track along this path are commonly associated with heavy snowfall in the regions bordering the Japan Sea. Put simply, the balmy tropical trade winds which had bought the *Hoop* and the *Liefde* quite swiftly to this point suddenly encountered a cold Arctic air mass blowing from the north. This was an environment where severe winter storms were generated, of the sort only previously encountered by the crews at the Magellan Strait.

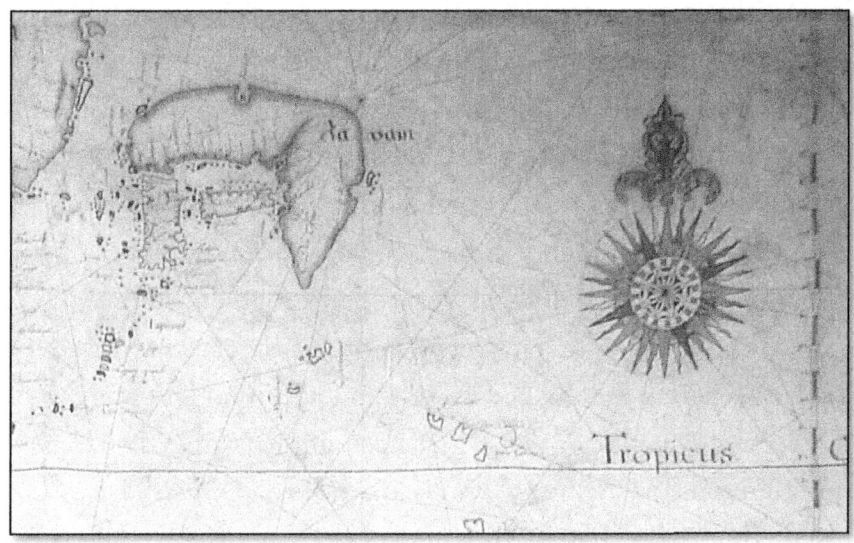

Figure 8. Detail from Doedsz' chart used by Adams to find Japan. The Isle of Una Colonna is shown just above the Tropic line – the southernmost of a small group of three islands. In the event of losing contact between the two ships, it was almost certainly agreed to meet off the supposed 'Southern Cape', at the latitude of $30°_N$, as indicated by the east-west parallel drawn through the centre of the compass rose.

Alone at sea now, the crew of the *Liefde* sought

desperately to regain control of their situation. Up until this point they had merely followed the lead of Timothy Shotten, the chief pilot of the *Hoop*. After searching awhile for their lost admiral, Quaeckernaeck and Adams resolved to do their best and head directly for Japan themselves, where they hoped to meet again with the *Hoop*. The rendezvous, already planned in case of such emergency, was an anchorage off the 'South Cape' of Japan at 30^0N, as shown on Cornelius Doedsz' map, and carried on both ships (Fig. 8). The storm had blown them severely off-route, however, pushing them away from Japan to the south and east. In making up lost sea-way they would have to battle more than just the northerly winter monsoon winds, and successive storms tracking eastward along the front, but also the contrary ocean current which flows west to east off Japan's southern shores. Named the *Kuroshio*, this powerful warm-water current flows all-year long, fueling both winter storms and late-summer typhoons with destructive energy. This final stage of the journey had to be fought for – against contrary winds and tides and with the ever-present knowledge that another storm may blow which could send them all to oblivion.

The South Cape, as represented on their charts was an obvious point for rendezvous, but the reality was that this supposedly prominent feature did not exist. Adams must have struggled to hold a position on latitude 30^0N, in thoroughly adverse conditions, looking for the cape and questioning his own

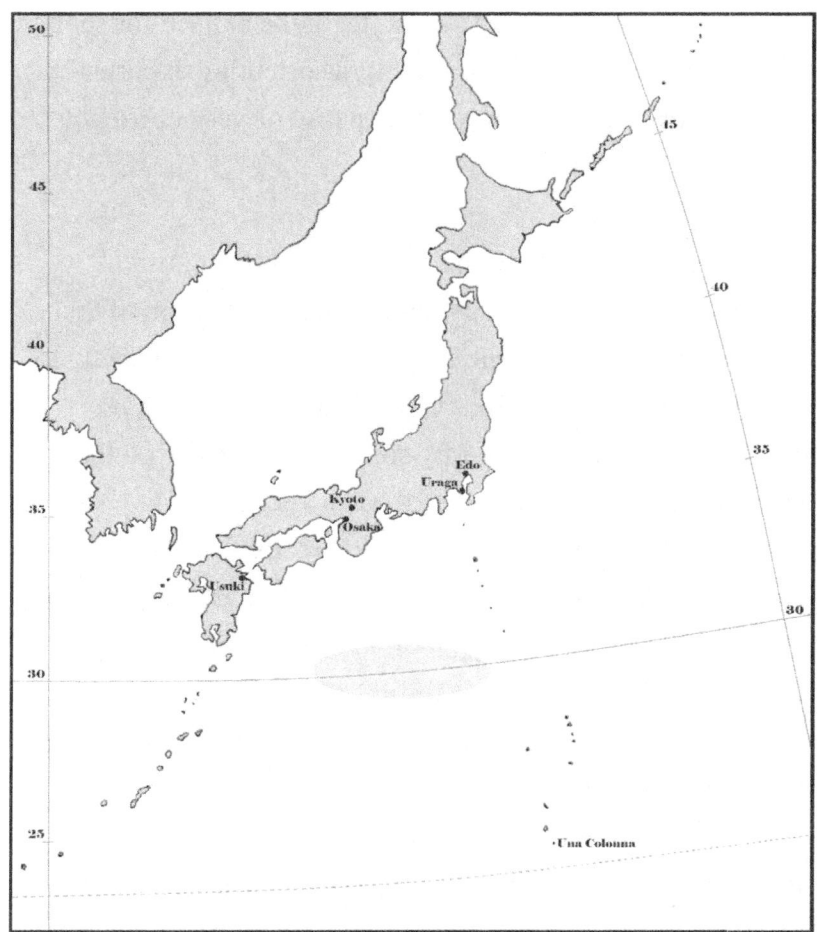

Figure 9: Modern map of Japan and surrounding area between longitude 125°$_E$ and 150°$_E$ highlighting the isle Adams calls Una Colonna. The dashed line represents the Tropic of Cancer, and the shaded zone is the approximate area Adams searched for the rendezvous point at the tip of the supposed 'South Cape'.

estimation of longitude. However far he sailed west, then east again, he could not find any land at all, let alone a place for shelter (Fig. 9). It must have been a thoroughly disorienting experience. He, the navigator, was lost - in a vast expanse of very unfriendly ocean.

Adams' solution required complete trust in his own abilities. Despite the risk that his longitudinal estimation of the ship's position was incorrect, he decided to retreat to the south, to a known and confirmed position on his chart, the isle of *Una Colonna*, which they had passed-by some weeks earlier on their northward passage. This small island has a very distinctive shape, being a near-perfect volcanic cone rising directly from the ocean. The peak is also the highest point for many miles around, and so could be readily spotted by sharp look-outs, even from many miles away. It is part of an archipelago of tiny isles and islets comprising what is known today as either the Bonin Islands or the Ogasawara Islands. Marked on his chart at a latitude around $24°30'_N$, *Una Colonna* is recognised around the world as one of the isles of Iwo-jima or, correctly, in recent years, as Io-tō. Doedsz' chart suggests, in fact, that it was Minami Io-tō, about 30 miles to the south of the main island of Io-tō (Iwo Jima).

It was with mixed feelings that Adams arrived there, recording in the letter to his wife:

"The foure and twentieth of March, we saw an island called Una Colonna; at which time many of our men were sicke

againe, and divers dead." (Purchas, 1625, Bk 3; 131)

The isle might have offered some respite but no refreshment, for there were no sheltered inlets on the coast of this small, steep-sided volcano for safe anchorage. The *Liefde* simply turned around once more, secure in the knowledge that a new bearing could be fixed with confidence. Adams' main concern was to get to the mainland of Japan. He was, by this time, probably in charge of the ship, his captain having fallen sick. In his own words:

"Great was the miserie we were in, having no more but nine or tenne able men to goe or creepe upon their knees: our Captaine, and all the rest, looking every houre to die" (ibid.).

At this time, having firmly re-established his location, he finally came to realise that the 'Southern Cape' he had sought in vain - in "the height of thirtie degrees", and subjected to "wind and weather" – did not exist. They had been misled:

"... by reason that it lieth false in all Chartes, and Globes, and Maps: for the Cape lyeth in thirtie five degrees $^1/_2$, which is a great difference" (Purchas, 1625 Bk 3; 126).

The latter reflection was written in 1611 and enjoyed the benefit of hindsight. $35^1/_2°N$ is the latitude in which Edo (Tokyo) is located – at the head of a bay. It is also the position of Cape Inubo (Chiba Prefecture), one of the most eastern promontories encountered by

Adams during his time in Japan. The tip of the Kii peninsula (Wakayama Prefecture), which is a likely candidate for the 'shrimp's tail' representing the South Cape on Doedsz' chart is actually found at approximately $33\frac{1}{2}°$N, over 200 miles away from the area Adams had been searching.

Discounting the false 'South Cape', Adams decided to seek an alternative destination where he could be certain of the accuracy of his charts, maps, and globe. He opted for the port of Usuki, on the east coast of the island of Kyushu in the former province of Bungo (now Oita Prefecture). Nagasaki might have been an alternative consideration but, given the sorry state of the *Liefde* and her crew, it was too far away – being on the west coast of Kyushu. Both Usuki and Nagasaki were ports where the Portuguese, as well as Jesuit missionaries, were known to have an established presence. However risky was the prospect of sailing into an 'enemy' harbor, Adams recognized that he had no alternative. For the sake of his surviving crew, as well as himself, he decided that the only hope for the expedition was to sail a direct course for Bungo, a journey that was to take almost three excruciating weeks.

Finally, land was sighted – being one of the four main islands of Japan. It is probable the island of Shikoku was seen before the island of Kyushu, off to starboard as the ship made slow but steady progress in a north-westerly direction. The going had become a little easier now as the influence of the winter monsoon waned and the wind took a more southerly direction. But, by now only a handful of the crew were left standing and tremendous effort was required to make any kind of headway. Exactly when land was first sighted is difficult to say. In Adams' letter to his wife he suggests it was the 11th April, and that they finally dropped anchor in Bungo Channel the following day (22nd April according to the Gregorian calendar)[39]. In his letter to 'Unknown Friends', he states it was the 19th April that they first saw land, and later, "now beinge in safetie", they came to an anchorage, perhaps a day or so later. Very precisely he states in the second letter they had been at sea for four months and twenty-two days since weighing anchor at the Isle of Santa Maria in Chile and dropping anchor in Japan. Clearly Adams had managed to keep an accurate log and was thus certain of the date of arrival, being the 21st April using the new-style calendar.

Towards the end of April, 1600, probably in the early morning of Friday 21st, the depleted crew of the *Liefde* would have seen the coast of Kyushu drifting by on their port side. At just above 33^{0}N, pilot William Adams turned to port and entered the Bungo Channel. Bounded on the northern flank by a narrow promontory pointing east, towards Shikoku, the ship was being guided inexorably towards the port and castle-town of Usuki (named Bungo by Adams, and Xativai by the Portuguese), at the far end of the bay. Slowly, and very carefully, Adams appraised the situation. On a modern ferry the journey into Usuki from this point takes about thirty minutes. First, he would have scanned the bay for any sign of the Admiral ship, the *Hoop*; lost to sight now for almost five weeks. The ship was not there. Instead, Adams observed that the port entrance was guarded by a strong fortification, perched on a hilltop, and surrounded by even stronger stone-built castle walls.

The Dutchman Dirck 'Pomp' Gerritsz, who had visited Japan previously and who had informed his friend Linschoten of the manners and customs of the Japanese people, had almost certainly spoken to Adams personally of his experiences there. Adams would have known, therefore, that Bungo/Usuki was one of the first harbours in Japan to have opened to Portuguese explorer-traders in the late 1540s. The local lord (*daimyō*) knew that the Portuguese were prepared to trade firearms, which before the Portuguese arrival in 1543 (at Tanegashima island) had been unknown in Japan. He was even prepared to convert to the Christian faith, as he intimated to Francis Xavier when the latter visited his castle in 1551, although he deferred his baptism until the year 1578[40].

Adams would also have known that since 1571 the main anchorage for Portuguese traders had become the excellent sheltered harbour of Nagasaki. It was a place subsequently organized and administered by the Jesuit priesthood, but they were restrained from excessive fervour by the appointment of two Japanese governors (*bugyō*). From time to time the Japanese asserted their authority, and it is probable Adams would not have known of the martyrdom of 26 Catholics by crucifixion there in February, 1597[41]. Nevertheless, he doubtless reasoned that, unlike encounters with indigenous peoples in the islands off equatorial Africa; in the Magellan Straight; in the coastal villages of Chile; and in the North Marianas islands, their reception in Japan would reflect a degree of Christian civility and so would not, necessarily, be potentially life-threatening[42]. Even if he did have doubts about making landfall here it was a gamble he simply had to take, for they could travel no further.

IX.   "...the people did us no harme, we not understanding each other, but by signes and tokens."[43]

Despite the cravings of the crew of the *Liefde* for food and sustenance Adams approached Usuki cautiously. He was, after all, sailing into 'enemy' territory where Portuguese influence was strong. In a scene that must have been reminiscent of the Marianas Islands they were soon confronted by many small boats coming out to them "the people whereof we willingly let come, having no force to resist them" (Purchas, 1625; Bk.3, 131). Perhaps taking care not to get too close to the fortress guarding the harbour, or perhaps not being able to proceed any further because of the press of boats around them, they finally dropped anchor in the lee of a small island called Kuroshima, about four miles (or 'one league' in Adams' words) from Usuki. Being only a few hundred yards from the mainland shore, however, the *Liefde* was soon swarming with curious local folk. With just twenty-four crew left alive, and with barely five men, including himself, "able to goe", they were in no position to hold back the swirl of people around them. As Adams suggests: "The people offered us no hurt". In fact, they were treated kindly and by use of sign language and the offer of various trinkets they received, in return, welcome refreshment. But, in the mayhem, almost every small and moveable item was stolen.

According to the Society of Jesus' account compiled by

Diogo de Couto and published years later in *Decada Duodecima*, two local Jesuit clerics were among the first to go out to the ship to offer aid, after first informing the authorities of the unexpected arrival. They feared the vessel was the annual ship from Luzon in the Philippines to Acapulco in New Spain (Mexico), perhaps blown off course in a storm but, as their boat got closer, they realized that this was not a "Catholic ship". Perhaps the carved sternpost, representing the figure of Erasmus, gave away the devotional allegiance of the crew, and the Jesuits immediately turned their boat around, to spread the news that Lutheran pirates had arrived. Once back on shore they sent a message to the headquarters of the Society in Nagasaki, to come and assist. The *daimyō* in this part of Bungo Province was Ōta Kazuyoshi, who would have been informed immediately of the strange arrival. After the former Christian *daimyō* of the whole province of Bungo, Ōtomo Sōrin, died in 1587, his son and successor Yoshimune fell out of favour and had been stripped of his possessions. In 1594 the province was subdivided into several much smaller territories, including Usuki. Ōta was a relatively minor lord, therefore, who was himself replaced by the end of the year, and whose only real claim to fame was that the crew of the *Liefde* arrived while he was still lord. Nevertheless, he was "King of that land" as far as both Adams *and* the Jesuits were concerned and carried the immediate authority that mattered so much to them. It was he, therefore, who ordered a troop of soldiers from the castle to gain control of the situation on the ship.

As far as is known, Lord Ōta was not a Christian *daimyō* (in the sense that he had been baptized), but he did tolerate the Jesuit presence in Usuki. He would not have felt any obligation to contact Nagasaki, therefore, unless it was to request help with translation, but he certainly *was* obliged to inform his own liege lords immediately of the sudden and unexpected arrival of foreigners. Indeed, all *daimyō*[44] around the country were under the same instruction, so a messenger was sent by fast galley to Osaka in central Japan. At this moment in time Japan was ruled by a Council of Regents, comprising five lords, from their mutual power-base at Osaka Castle. Lord Ōta could not make any decisions regarding the fate of Adams and his crew-mates until he had a reply from the Council, or at least one of the Regents. In the meantime, he was obliged to protect the men of the *Liefde* and offer all reasonable comfort for the crew and aid for the sick.

The first task was to bring the ship into Usuki harbour, probably by towing the vessel with row-boats on a rising tide. This must have been done the next day, for another three of the crew had died during the night. Lord Ōta would have been fearful of losing all these men before his superiors had the chance to interview them. In the harbour all the men transferred to shore, some making their own way and others being carried, and were taken to a house made which had been made available by the *daimyō*. There they could rest and, of course, they were fed and refreshed. Yet despite all this care another three men died before making any kind of recovery; a testament to the extremely dire situation the ship was in prior to arrival in Japan.

Eighteen crew were to survive, including a seemingly disproportionate number of ships' officers, including the captain, Adams, and the ships' carpenter, as well as merchant-mariners representing the Rotterdam Company. This probably reflects not so much on better nutrition enjoyed by these people on the voyage (in the latter stages all shared what little was available) but conditions in the living quarters on board ship. Infectious disease was more likely to spread in the unhygienic conditions of the crowded sailors' quarters than in the cabins allocated to senior members of the crew. Notwithstanding, the captain, Jacob Quaekernaek was seriously, but not fatally, ill. The spokesperson for the entire crew would be the next most senior officer – the navigator - William Adams.

The crew received several visitors during the first few days, including the merely inquisitive as well as those tasked with working out what to do with the unexpected new arrivals. Given the relatively long history of Catholicism in Usuki there were local acolytes who would have had some understanding of the Portuguese language, and who may have made the first attempts at meaningful conversation with Adams and his fellow sea-farers. Since Adams could 'get by' using Spanish, it would not be long before the local population knew that they were hosts to a group of Dutch merchants looking for the opportunity to trade. Equally, the crew would have been told that no change in their presently comfortable situation would happen until word came back from the "...principall King of the whole Island", dictating the next sequence of events. But, after about a week or so, all signs of congeniality changed suddenly - for the worse:

"After we had beene there five or sixe days, came a Portugall Jesuite with other Portugals, who reported of us, that we were Pirats, and were not in the way of Marchandizing. Which report caused the Governour and common-people to think evill of us: In such manner, that we looked always when we should be set upon Crosses; which is the execution in this land for theevery and some other crimes. Thus daily more and more the Portugalls incensed the Justices and people against us." (Purchas, 1625; Bk.3, 131).

Messages had been dispatched hot-foot to Nagasaki about the arrival of a strange western vessel, and the priests there had wasted no time at all to get back to Usuki and investigate the foreign intruders; a journey which normally would take three or four days each way overland. The Jesuits did not welcome non-Catholic strangers!

Before setting out for Usuki the Portuguese Jesuits had written to Lord Terazawa, the *daimyō* of Hizen Province and a governor of the special status town of Nagasaki, warning him of the Dutch pirates: "the enemies of the Portuguese and of all Christians." Unbeknown to the Jesuits, Terazawa was at this time being dispatched by Lord Tokugawa, one of the Regents in Osaka, to Usuki, with instructions to convey the ship and its crew to Osaka (Schütte, 1980; 219). Under normal circumstances, Lord Terazawa would have no authority over affairs in Usuki, but on this occasion his word would be supreme, and his instructions from Osaka were to make sure no harm befell the crew of the *Liefde*. All this was, of course, not yet clear to anyone in Usuki when the party from Nagasaki arrived there. The Jesuit delegation had found Lord Ōta was at least prepared to listen to their fears and certainly had no hesitation allowing his Portuguese guests to tour the *Liefde*, and to make an inventory of all the items in the hold. This list is reproduced in *Decada*:

"Eleven large chests containing coarse woolen fabric; a small crate with 400 coral necklaces and bracelets, and just as many made from amber; a box with pieces of coloured glass, and some mirrors and spectacles; many children's trumpets; 2000 *cruzados* **in** *reals* (gold coins); **nineteen heavy bronze cannon, and other light ones; 500 muskets, and 5000 cast-iron shot, and 300 chain-shot; 50 quintals of powder; three boxes with chain-mail, and three with breast-plates and cuirasses; 350 fire-arrows; many nails, much iron; many axes, scythes and mattocks, and various other kinds of tools"** - followed by the comment: **"…with which they obviously came for conquest and to establish settlements."** (de Couto, 1645; reprinted in Wieder, 1925; Vol.3, 130-131)

The Jesuits' collective clerical advice to Lord Ōta was offered straight away. First, being a Dutch ship, it was clear that the crew were Protestants, and therefore heretics in the eyes of God. Second, the disproportionately large number of arms and munitions carried on the ship led to the obvious conclusion that they were pirates rather than honest merchants. On both these grounds all the crew should be put to death with immediate effect. Interrogations seemed hardly necessary.

The leader of the Jesuit delegation from Nagasaki was João Rodrigues, also called Tçuzzi, indicating he was 'the interpreter'. He was known to Lord Tokugawa, and trusted by him and, over the following years, would become well-known to Adams too. He wrote of his discourses in Bungo to his superior in Nagasaki, Alexandre Valignano, who subsequently reported all this to his own superiors in Macao (Schütte, 1980; 213). As might be expected, his own account and that of Adams concerning what happened in Usuki vary in terms of the emphasis each one of them places on events as they unfolded. When the Portuguese delegation did finally speak to the crew of the *Liefde* both he and Adams agree that the objective was to impart information rather than conduct an inquisition. Nevertheless, Adams would have tried his damnedest to point out that there were absolutely no Portuguese or Spanish goods on board, and that there was no proof whatsoever of piracy. The armaments carried were purely for defense, or for sale; and the accusation of heresy was absolute nonsense.

But, by Adams' account, the Jesuit leader having already made judgement announced that in his esteemed opinion the intruders were indeed pirates and heretics, and so should be subject to the most appropriate method the Japanese authorities had devised for execution of the perpetrators of such crimes: crucifixion. Thievery at sea had been a damaging issue for all East Asian dominions since the peak of *wako* (local pirate) activity in the mid-16th century, and punishment regimes were the severest possible[45]. Crucifixion, Japanese-style, was an excruciating form of death facing all sea-thieves (and Christians too, in times of prohibition), and some of the group of Portuguese from Nagasaki seemed to relish telling the weakened crew of the *Liefde* exactly how they would die. Roped to crossed pieces of wood; arms and legs spread akimbo; and the cross raised high for all to see the victim; lances would be inserted under one side of the rib-cage; then pushed and twisted and tweaked until the tips of the weapons appeared between the opposite shoulder and neck, next to the face of the screaming victim. They would be skewered, slowly. Ideally, the first lance would not bring about death, because the skill of the executioner was demonstrated by his ability to avoid the heart and other vital organs while pushing the spear-tip through the torso. So, a second lance would be shoved in from the other side, providing another shape of the cross.

According to João Rodrigues, it was only the Japanese authorities who were highly suspicious of the ship and her crew, and he was merely explaining the Japanese position to them. He could not help but explain to them the dangers they were in. As a religious man, he could never wish them any harm and, indeed, felt in danger himself for simply associating with them as an intermediary (Schütte, 1980; 215). Not so often recounted are the memories he held, vividly, and with genuine compassion, of the 26 martyrs of Nagasaki who had all been 'crossed' just three years previously. Rodrigues had stood at the feet of each of the victims as they perished, trying to comfort their thoughts and offer a route for the salvation of their souls as they passed, on their terrible and tortuous path to the afterlife (Cooper, 2001; *xvii*).

Whatever the feelings Rodrigues had conveyed, that night Adams and his fellow crew members were left to ruminate on their fate. Despite the fact they were, on the whole, being well-treated and looked-after, the group suspected that they were effectively under house-arrest and subject to the whim of the Lord of Usuki. They had also witnessed the influence of both local and Portuguese Jesuits over the local populace and so feared, not just for their lives, but the shocking way in which they would lose them. Two of the crew were so badly affected during that night that, next morning, they turned on their comrades – "as traytors" - and:

"… gave themselves in service to the King, being all in all with the Portugals, having by them their lives warranted. The one was called *Gilbert de Conning*, whose mother dwelleth at

Middleborough, who gave himselfe out to be Marchant of all the goods in the Shippe. The other was called *John Abelson Van Owater*. These traitours sought all manner of wayes to get the goods into their hands, and made knowne unto them all things that had passed in our voyage." (Purchas, 1625; Bk.3, 131).

The events of that day can be imagined readily. The remaining crew-members were clearly furious at their former 'comrades' and more than likely had to be restrained from any attempt to inflict serious harm. Their hosts must have acted quickly to prevent complete chaos ensuing. Then, within a day or two, according to Adams, an emissary, Lord Teruzawa, arrived from the court at Osaka; borne, impressively, by a fleet of five galleys. One of these was to return immediately with the captain of the *Liefde* but, since Quaeckernaeck was too sick to travel, Adams would go in his stead. He recalled that:

"Nine dayes after our arrival, the great King of the land sent for me to come unto him. So taking one man with me, I went to him, taking leave of our Captaine, and all the others that were sicke, commending my selfe into his hands, that had preserved me from so many perils on the sea. I was carried in one of the Kings gallies to the Court at *Osaca*, where the King lay, about eightie leagues from the place where the Shippe was. The twelfth of May, 1600. I came to the great Kings citie: …" (ibid.).

Once again, Adams became confused with his conversion from Gregorian to Julian calendars in the letter to his wife, and got the date seriously wrong, stating 12th May instead of 22nd April[46]. The new-style date of his arrival at Osaka was probably 2nd May, 1600.

Japanese records on this are scanty and somewhat ambiguous but seem to suggest that the order to summons Adams to Osaka was issued on 29th April, probably the same day that the galleys were dispatched (Dainihonshiryō, 11-913; 217). It seems Terazawa had indeed been dispatched from Osaka (rather than his own territory in northern Kyushu), for his troops were later to march with those of Tokugawa to Edo, even further to the east. Of the five galleys sent to Usuki, all would have had a single bank of at least ten oars on either side, below the main deck, and were remarkably fast. Some of them may have had a wooden cabin superstructure, to accommodate passengers in reasonable comfort. These ships were known as *sekibune*. The other type of vessel, known as *kohaya* (literally: 'small and fast'), had an open, but slightly raised main deck, providing a platform for archers. They were the 'work-horses' of the military fleet and were a common sight on the Inland Sea across which Adams had to be taken to get to Osaka. The reason for sending as many as five galleys was to send Japanese mariners who could secure the foreign ship, and eventually help move her and the rest of the crew as well.

The journey from Usuki could be done easily within two

days. There is no doubt Adams was accompanied on the fast voyage to Osaka by one individual, but the identification of this other person is open to question. The tone Adams uses in his letter to his wife clearly suggests the man was of lower rank and authority. Indeed, in his other letter, to 'Unknown Friends', he describes how, after his arrival in Osaka, he was "…with one of our Mariners, that came with me to serve me". This would imply that Adams was still being treated as an honoured guest and was being granted all due respect. No further mention is made of the man in Adams' letters, which are the only-known accounts of these proceedings, but Dutch tradition has it that he was Jan Joosten, a merchant who, at the very least, would have regarded himself as Adams' equal, if not his social superior. Years later, Jan Joosten would share the honour granted to William Adams of being created a *hatamoto* samurai[47].

Osaka was a city on a scale rivalling, if not surpassing that of the ancient capital of Kyoto. It was located near the mouth of the estuary of the Yodo River, guarding access not just to Kyoto, a few hours' journey further north by river-boat, but also to the capital's hinterland and indeed, to the heartland of the country itself. Just beyond Kyoto, another boat could be taken to cross Lake Biwa, to access routes leading to the Japan Sea coast, or to the provinces of northern Japan. Osaka was therefore the gateway to the interior, and main hub of the trading network which extended via coastal sea-ways, rivers, and highways across all Japan. Unfortunately, trade had been inhibited by protracted periods of civil war and unrest, lasting many centuries, and remembered in Japanese history as the period of Warring States. The last thirty years had seen encouraging signs of the re-emergence of a strong, centralized state, but the continuing need for military might was characterized in Osaka by the construction of a castle and massive fortifications just sixteen years prior to Adams' arrival there. Built by one of the principal unifiers of the country, Toyotomi Hideyoshi, Osaka castle was the epitome of his remarkable talent for military strategic planning, combined with a new-style urban design.

Unfortunately, the *Taikō*, as Hideyoshi was known, had died less than two years previously, in September, 1598, leaving a son aged only five as successor. The son, Hideyori, had subsequently been installed in Osaka castle, together with his mother, and a council of five regents to govern the country during the years of minority. In this sense, Osaka, and a small number of other castles in Japan, held the function of being the base for national government, rather than a provincial headquarters for individual provincial *daimyō*. The Council was represented by the most powerful *daimyō* in the land, who each derived their incomes from the territories they possessed in the provinces, and inevitable frictions between them were mounting by the day. Continuation of the civil war seemed inevitable, despite the checks Hideyoshi had put in place to ensure this did not occur. As things happened, probably by contrivance, only one of the regents was presently in residence at the castle, the others having returned to their own provinces to prepare, if necessary, for a final, decisive battle. It was Lord Tokugawa Ieyasu, therefore, who had summoned Adams to appear before him at Osaka, and whom Adams referred to as the "principall King".

X. *"Comming before the King, he viewed me well, and seemed to be wonderfull favourable."*[48]

Wasting no time, Adams was taken directly to the outer walls of Osaka castle where they were closest to the river. It was late afternoon, and cherry blossom blown by a stiff, but gusty breeze gave the appearance of a wintry storm under a bright blue sky. Crossing the broad outer moat by a wooden bridge he faced a formidable gated-entrance, with massively thick wooden doors studded and decorated with iron. Beyond loomed the lacquer-blacked seven-storied central keep, but this time the elaborately shaped roof structures were highlighted in gold, and the otherwise ominous and awe-inspiring building twinkled and glittered in the sun. Through the barred window openings of the gateway, and the arrow slits and rounded musket firing-holes set into the walls beyond, Adams was aware that he was being watched keenly by troops of breast-plated guards. Glancing away, along the moat, the stone walls seemed to stretch away endlessly into the distance, all constructed of massive, but neatly hewn granite boulders. The 'king' was clearly a man of considerable power.

Led by their escort, Adams and his fellow crew member went through the gate and then headed away from the direction of the keep. It was surrounded by a series of sprawling enclosures, and in the largest of these, named Nishi-no-maru, he was taken to a smaller gateway set in a neat plaster and tiled wall. Beyond was a large compound containing a finely constructed residential mansion and a series of related outbuildings. This was the headquarters, as well as private quarters, of the regent (*Tairō*) Tokugawa Ieyasu, for the times he was on official duty at Osaka castle (Dainihonshiryō, 1974; 11-913, 223). All the regents had similar compounds (called *yashiki*), as well as some members of the Toyotomi family. The young son and heir of the *Taikō*, Hideyori, resided in a palace near to the keep, whilst formal affairs of state were carried out in a separate palatial structure in the main courtyard (*honmaru*). Since Ieyasu was the sole regent currently residing in the castle, it was appropriate that Adams be interviewed in his own quarters and, in any case, it suited him best if he, and he alone, gained the knowledge he sought, even if under the auspices of Council affairs. Carrying maps, charts, and a globe they had brought with them from the ship, Adams and his companion were guided to an unfurnished ante-room and invited to sit on two plush cushions placed on the *tatami*-matted floor. Offered light refreshments, they could only sit and wait while Ieyasu was informed of their presence.

Lord Tokugawa would have taken time to finish whatever business he was engaged in. Being a meticulous man, and a brilliant strategist, he would have taken even more time to read or listen to intelligence reports from the officers who had just returned from Usuki, and certainly would have been made aware of the full inventory of all the items carried on the *Liefde*. Only then would he have gone, together with an adviser and assistant or secretary, to the private audience chamber, arranging himself, sitting comfortably on a kind of armchair without legs, atop a slightly raised dias, to witness the entry of his guests. Adams, appearing from behind a sliding screen door at the far end of the austere but tastefully decorated chamber, would have been struck immediately by the sense of awe and respect the elderly, greying man opposite him commanded. With some trepidation the pair approached, bowing as they went, until it was indicated firmly that they should kneel on the *tatami* covered floor. As Adams recalled events of that day later:

"I came to the great Kings citie: who caused me to be brought into the Court, being a wonderfull costly house guilded with gold in abundance. Comming before the King, he viewed me well, and seemed to be wonderfull favourable. He made many signes unto me, some of which I understood, and some I did not. In the end there came one that could speake Portuges. By him the King demanded of me, of what Land I was, and what mooved us to come to his Land beeing so farre off." (Purchas, 1625; Bk 3, 131)

Ieyasu would surely have smiled inwardly at the somewhat comic appearance of the two foreigners. Dressed in unfamiliar and ill-fitting attire (almost certainly they were wearing cotton gowns given to them in Usuki), and totally uncertain about the strict etiquette required to be followed on such an occasion, they no doubt fumbled with Adams' globe and charts as they tried to kneel whilst maintaining a sense of decorum.

The cumbersome maps actually proved to be a godsend. Ieyasu spoke only in Japanese, a language Adams had absolutely no comprehension of. While waiting for the interpreter to arrive, however, it was the simplest of matters for Adams to unfurl a chart; tap himself on the chest and point his finger at England and the provinces of the Netherlands. Tracing the route they had followed to Japan, Ieyasu smiled openly and was pleased; he loved poring over maps. As Adams noted:

"As (to) what way we came to the Country. Having a Chart of the whole world, I shewed him, through the *Straight of Magellan*. At which he wondred, and thought me to lie." (ibid.)

Even without the interpreter the interview soon became animated. "But it *is* true!" he might well have mimed, pointing to the globe and the chart by Hondius where the routes through the Strait of Magellan taken by both Drake and Cavendish were clearly marked.

At this point Pedro Morejón arrived to act as interpreter. He had been summoned, in haste, from the Jesuit Society House where he was the senior priest. The House was located just outside the castle walls, in the quarter for high-ranking samurai, overlooking the river (Schütte, 1980; 221-222). Discussion of the charts continued, with Adams' retelling of the stories of Barentsz,

Frobisher, and Davis, and their quests to discover a northern passage to Japan. Morejón, who was clearly the source for the later Portuguese account which appeared in *Decada*, confused this aspect of Adams tale with the thought that Adams was recounting his *own* journeys of exploration. But Ieyasu really wanted to know *why* Adams had made the perilous voyage across two oceans; what were his motives? Why were other countries so interested in Japan?

By way of answer, according to Adams:

"I shewed unto him the name of our Countrey, and (explained) **that our land had long sought out the East-Indies, and desired friendship with all Kings and Potentates in way of marchandize, having in our Land diverse commodities, which these Lands had not."** (ibid.)

Then all sorts of questions followed, and: "… I answered him in all points, for there was nothing that he demanded not, both concerning warre, and peace between Countrey and Countrey …" (Purchas, 1625; Bk.3, 126). Elaborating on this, according to the letter to his wife:

"Then he asked whether our Countrey had warres. I answered him yea, with the Spaniards and Portugals, being in peace with all other Nations. Further, he asked me in what did I beleeve? I said in God that made Heaven and Earth." (Purchas, 1625; Bk

3, 131)

Ieyasu was probing, being fully aware of the possibility that Christian evangelism could be a precursor to aggression by a foreign nation. His predecessor, the *Taikō*, had already been warned against Spanish intentions in this respect. He probably did not expect, however, the answers he received.

Until now, Ieyasu's knowledge of European affairs was based entirely on an Iberian perspective. As Massarella puts it, the Spanish mendicant friars and Portuguese Jesuit priests had enjoyed a 'monopoly of information' when it came to describing foreign affairs in faraway lands; all was love and peace in a unitary Catholic world (Massarella, 1990; 78). Adams was now telling him, for the first time, that both nations were at war with other nations who *really* desired peace and trade with kingdoms such as Japan. The Spanish and Portuguese peoples even harboured notions of conflict with one another, in a Europe comprising Christian nations themselves split between Catholic and Protestant interpretations of the faith. This was very useful information indeed for Ieyasu, who was at this time nurturing ideas of peaceful trade between Japan and all other friendly nations.

Time was moving on quickly, however, and much information had already been imparted. As Adams continues:

"Thus from one thing to another I abode with him till mid-

night. And having asked mee what marchandize we had in our shippe, I shewed him all. In the end, he beeing ready to depart, I desired that we might have trade of marchandize, as the Portugals and the Spanyards had. To which he made me an answer, but what it was I did not understand." (ibid.)

In fact, the interview, or interrogation was not over yet. Although Adams felt that everything had gone well, Ieyasu intended more hard questioning, to see if Adams could be caught out with any kind of inappropriate response. In the meantime, he wished to remind Adams and his companion of the precariousness of the position they were in, despite having warmed to them somewhat. So, he commanded that the two be sent to a prison – "being well used" - according to Adams' letter to 'Unknown Friends'. The jail would have been the one in common use, set somewhere within the castle walls to house any citizen arrested for any perceived misdemeanor. Most likely it was in the lower part of the expansive castle compound, in a small enclosure where there was a constant presence of armed soldiers. Also, rather than resembling a dungeon it was probably a large wooden cage, with no facilities, open on at least two or three sides for all to see the occupants within, through the wooden bars. From time to time an occupant would be taken away for interrogation by a magistrate, and buckets containing water and gruel for common consumption placed inside. Unable to communicate with anyone but his crewmate, Adams could only contemplate his likely fate, and think of crucifixion once more.

Their misery lasted two nights and a day. During the second day Adams was summoned again to Ieyasu's *yashiki* and further questioned by him. The tone was serious as Ieyasu asked once more for the reason why, exactly, he had come to Japan, travelling so far, and experiencing such great hardship. His answer was diplomatic and, presumably speaking from both the English and Dutch perspectives, answered that:

"We were a People that sought all friendship with all Nations, and so have trade of Merchandize in all Countries, bringing such Merchandizes as our Country had, and buying such Merchandizes in strange Countryes, as our Countrey desired, through which our Countryes on both side were inriched." (Purchas, 1625; Bk.3, 127)

Ieyasu also returned to the question of war with the Spanish and Portuguese and asked what the nature of this war was and what were the reasons for it. Again, given the wide breadth of topics that Ieyasu appeared interested in, it would seem the interview lasted several hours. As Adams summarized the meeting in the letter to his wife, Ieyasu:

"…enquired of the qualities and conditions of our Countreys, of Warres and Peace, of Beasts and Cattel of all sorts, of the Heavens. It seemed that he was well content with all mine answers unto his demands." (Purchas, 1625; Bk.3, 132)

Unfortunately, this is the last event Adams describes in the surviving part of the letter to Mary, his wife. It concludes: "Nevertheless, I was commanded to prison againe, but my lodging was bettered in another place."

It seems Adams and his 'servant' were kept under a form of house-arrest after the second interview, probably in some form of accommodation separate from Ieyasu's residence, but inside the same compound that had been allocated to Ieyasu in the western bailey of the castle. All *yashiki* used by a major lord such as Tokugawa Ieyasu would incorporate a detached single-storied *nagaya*, or long-house, providing accommodation usually reserved as quarters for soldiers or servants. Divided into a series of separate, but small rooms, facilities were basic but did at least offer a small degree of privacy to each occupant. They would not be aware of Ieyasu's movements, or even see him, but he could rest assured that they were secure and cared for, and out of the way of prying eyes. Adams was to spend over a month here and, since he was clearly not languishing in a prison environment, he was probably visited from time to time by Morejón to make sure he understood any instructions given him by his jailers - if nothing else.

Visits by an interpreter could not allay Adams' fears, however, and may even have exasperated them. As each day passed there was no news of what was to happen to the pair of them, nor of what might have befallen their crew-mates. Certainly, Morejón could not enlighten them, but was, perhaps, in a position to let them know what his Jesuit colleagues were up to. In his letter to 'Unknown Friends', Adams described his perceptions of what was going on:

"...I looked every day to be *Crossed*, as the custome of Justice is in *Japan*, as hanging is in our Land. Now in this long time of imprisonment, the Jesuites and the Portugals gave many evidences to the Emperour against us, alleadging that wee were theeves and robbers against all Nations, and if we were suffered to live, it should be against the profit of his Majestie, and the Land: for then no Nation could come there without robbing: but if Justice were executed on us, it would terrifie the rest of our Nation from coming there any more. And to this intent they sued to his Majestie daily to cut us off, making all the friends they could to this purpose." (Purchas, 1625; Bk.3, 127)

Ieyasu, whom Adams invariably describes as 'Emperor', 'King', or 'Majesty', had much else on his mind, however. He was thinking above all of the impending war, in which he would have to confront at least two of his fellow regents. The time for diplomatic nicety was over, although he did spare time at the end of the month for a five-day visit to Fushimi castle, near Kyoto, for a series of meetings with other *daimyō*. Fushimi castle, which had also been built by the *Taikō,* Hideyoshi, and which had been his main residence, remained at the centre of political affairs in Japan, together with Osaka castle. Ieyasu was managing to maintain an air of normality, therefore. Shortly after his return to Osaka, on 3rd June, he heard news concerning the arrival of the *Liefde* in the port of Sakai, a few miles to the south. He knew that now was the time to decide Adams' fate.

Without doubt, Ieyasu had wanted to secure possession of the Dutch ship because of the armaments she carried, so he had ordered that the *Liefde* should be brought to Sakai as soon as the surviving crew had recovered. This also provided an opportunity to corroborate Adams' story, and to determine from the evidence now at hand whether his execution might be justified. Adams himself was counting the days of his present confinement, stating that he "…continued nine and thirty dayes in prison, hearing no more newes, neither of our ship, nor Captaine, whether he were recovered of his sicknesse, nor of the rest of the company…" (ibid.). Then, around 12th June, Adams was summoned to Ieyasu's private audience chamber once more. His mind was immediately put at ease when Ieyasu explained that since Adams had come peacefully and had shown no intent to harm either himself or any of the Japanese people, that it was "against all reason and justice" to order him to be put to death, as the Jesuit priests had demanded. He added that it was no real concern of his if Adams' own nation was at a state of war with other nations, if conflict stayed beyond the shores of Japan.

As can be imagined, Adams must have breathed a huge sigh of relief, while the interpreter who conveyed this news must have fought hard to hide his own reaction to it. The interview continued with yet more questions asked of Adams, suggesting that Ieyasu had a genuine interest in the knowledge he possessed, and a desire to learn yet more. After a while, Ieyasu enquired:

"…whether I was desirous to goe to the ship to see my Countrey-men: I answered, that I would very gladly do it: soe he bade me goe. Then I departed, and was freed from imprisonment." (ibid.)

XI. *"…all we that were left alive, came together again."*

So, on the "one and fortieth day" he had been in Osaka castle, Adams and his crew-mate were led back to the boat dock, for transfer to Sakai:

"Wherefore, with a rejoycing heart I tooke a Boat, and went to our ship, where I found the Captaine and the rest, recovered of their sicknesse. But at our meeting aboord, we saluted one another with mourning and sheadding of teares: for they were informed that I was executed, and long since dead. Thus, God be praised, all we that were left alive, came together again." (Purchas, 1625; Bk.3, 127)

From this point onward, for the next few months, the only account of the events that happened is in Adams' letter to 'Unknown Friends'. In that letter, his first observation following the crew reunion was that "All things were taken out of the ship…" (ibid.). He continues, noting that all his personal possessions, including his navigational instruments, and even all his spare clothes had disappeared, and that the same was true for all the other crew. The ship had, essentially, been stripped bare. The manner in which he writes of this is somewhat ambiguous, however. He clearly states that Ieyasu had no idea of the losses of personal effects but is not so clear about responsibility for the removal of all the cargo. Also, does he mean that all the ship's armaments had been taken as well? He wrote:

"All things were taken out of the ship, together with all my instruments, &c. and I had nothing left me, but my clothes on my backe: likewise whatsoever the rest of the company had, was also taken away, unknowne to the Emperour: which when he understood, he gave order that they should be restored to us againe. But being so dispersed abroad, they could not be had; yet fiftie thousand rials in ready money were commanded to be given us, the Emperour himself seeing the delivery thereof to the hands of one that was made our Governour, who kept them in his hands to distribute them unto us as wee had neede, for the buying of Victualls for our men, with other particular charges &c." (ibid.)

A certain amount of pilfering had gone on when the *Liefde* first arrived in Japan, and doubtless continued to some extent when the crew were recovering ashore at Usuki. What Adams describes, however, seems to have been more systematic and can only have taken place with the knowledge of the crew, especially if the losses included all the cargo and armaments. Blame cannot be laid with Lord Ōta in Usuki, for he was a Hideyoshi loyalist and would not have risked upsetting the Council of Regents in any way. The ship must have been brought to Sakai replete with most of its goods, therefore, and certainly with all the cannon, muskets, and gunpowder it had brought to Japan.

Clearly, Ieyasu had appointed a loyal retainer to act as "Governour" of the ship and crew, and to ensure the safety and security of all. An armed-guard would have been placed around the ship, and on the quayside, keeping 24-hour watch. Most likely the Japanese official had been ordered to find accommodation for the crew ashore, and only then arranged for the ship to be completely cleared of *everything* remaining aboard. Ieyasu had plenty of contacts within the merchant community in the city and could easily have arranged to place all the goods, including the armaments, discretely in dry storage in a nearby empty warehouse. When the crew returned to the ship, prior to the re-union with Adams, they would, of course, have been aware that everything was now missing, but their bemusement would be met with a simple shoulder-shrug. The bottom-line was that, as far as the Dutch were concerned, on arrival in Sakai everything had been 'sold' for the princely sum of 50,000 pieces of silver – non-negotiable!

According to Alexandre Valignano, who was the Jesuit superior in Nagasaki who compiled the report (still extant) which eventually formed the basis of the story in *Decada* concerning Adams and the Jesuits, he obtained his information directly by letter from Pedro Morejón. Whilst this letter no longer exists, Valignano did quote passages from it. Morejón is thus reputed to have claimed to have met Adams in Osaka (Sakai) at the house where the crew were staying. Moreover, he suggests that this is where Adams took the time to explain his charts, and all the other things that he had so carefully related to Ieyasu already (Schütte, 1980; 222). This is nonsense because, even if Morejón had been admitted to the house, it would have been for a few uncomfortable minutes at most, and not the hours required to tell the whole story. Adams, in a letter he wrote in 1613 to August Spalding stated very clearly that "…the Spanyard and Portingall hath bin my bitter ennemis to death…", and would not have tolerated his presence for long, if at all, so soon after his imprisonment (Farrington, 1991; 77). Perhaps Morejón was referring to the *nagaya*, where Adams had been kept under house-arrest, but even there, such a lengthy discussion was unlikely to have happened. It is clear Morejón concocted, or at least exaggerated his story, to obscure the fact that he had obtained the information while acting in good faith as interpreter on behalf of Lord Tokugawa. In other words, this was information he had no right to share.

One of the great debates circulating around the story of William Adams concerns the fate of the cannon from the *Liefde* and, given that Adams was later credited with teaching the art of gunnery to Ieyasu, whether he and those guns later played a role in the decisive fight that Ieyasu was undoubtedly preparing for; the Battle of Sekigahara (see Rogers, 2016; 71). Adams first-hand involvement in the battle is highly unlikely, and if Ieyasu wanted no part in Adams' wars, why would he expect Adams to take part in his? The weapons taken from the ship had now been paid for, and Ieyasu was free to dispose of them as he wished. In fact.

production of firearms, and of gunpowder, was already well-developed in Japan, and there was a history of their deployment in battle. The arquebus, or musket, was most effectively deployed as a defensive weapon, even in open battle, and the standing armies of most of the major *daimyō* contained at least one detachment of trained arquebusiers. Ieyasu would certainly have been happy to supply 500 new muskets to his personal troops or, alternatively, to the garrison at Fushimi castle who would also be fighting on his side.

The nineteen great guns brought on the *Liefde* were cumbersome and lacked the mobility required for open battle, however, and logistical reasons alone would dissuade Ieyasu from deploying them on a fast-moving campaign. They were most effective in static warfare, such as a castle siege, for both attackers and defenders. Ieyasu knew that the Fushimi castle garrison would remain loyal to him and could play a crucial role in holding up any advance from western Japan where most of those who opposed him were based. It would make most sense, therefore, to transfer the ship's cannon to Fushimi, for the anticipated defense of the castle where particularly effective use could be made of the store of chain-shot and fire-arrows. In fact, all the guns, shot, and powder could be transferred there by boat from Sakai, while maintaining a reasonable degree of secrecy. The only other option was to keep the armaments on-board the *Liefde*, and transfer them with the ship and crew to Ieyasu's feudal base at Edo. There is no record to suggest this happened, however, and when the ship finally did make the journey to Kanto it must have eased Ieyasu's mind to have a large, *unarmed* foreign vessel entering Edo Bay.

Jacob Quaeckernaeck now had an opportunity to reflect on the new circumstances he and the crew found themselves in. Since all short-term requirements were now met, and the crew were fed and clothed – and together, sleeping on the ship – he considered the longer term. He was obliged to seek merchandize to purchase, looking for goods that could be either traded in the Spice Islands, or sold for profit back in Rotterdam. He might not have known it, but Sakai was exactly the right place to be; it was the trade emporium of Japan. He also had the money to do this, but only if cash was released by the official placed in-charge of them all, and it seems he was not authorized to allow such purchases. Frustratingly, his reply would always have been that he would have to consult with Ieyasu. Eventually, after one month, word did come back from Osaka castle:

"…commandement came from the Emperour, that our ship should be carried to the Easter part of the land, called *Quanto*, whither according to his commandement we were carried, the distance being about an hundred and twenty leagues. Our passage thither was long by reason of contrary windes, so that the Emperour was there long before us." (ibid.).

That the *Liefde* was 'carried' to Kantō clearly indicates that even though Quaeckernaeck was captain, he was not in charge. The choice of destination, the course to take, and the crewing of the ship was all in Japanese hands, under the direction of "the Governour". They departed Sakai in mid-July, well into the summer season when the weather became hot and sultry. A lack of wind rather than contrary winds was the most likely reason for slow progress, but it was always a possibility that a typhoon could appear from the south-west at this time of year. With this in mind, the Japanese crew seems to have adopted a very cautious approach, anchoring in any port or haven en route to ensure safe passage. For Adams, with nothing else to do, it was an opportunity to observe the Japanese coast, and possibly draw some sketches. It seems he still had his globe and charts, even if his navigational instruments were missing, and on one of them – the Indian Ocean chart – it appears that he attempted to re-draw the shape of the coastline. He knew his charts were "false", particularly around the supposed 'Southern Cape', so from simple observation alone he attempted to correct this[49]. It was a crude attempt, handicapped by lack of instruments, but his basic representation of the major capes and bays encountered en route was accurate.

Ieyasu himself left Osaka castle on 26th July. The day before, he had entertained the young son of the *Taikō*, Toyotomi Hideyori, at his residence in the castle in *Nishi-no-maru* (the western enclosure) and been presented with the handsome sum of 20,000 *koku* (a measure of wealth in Japan representing, perhaps, the annual income of a lesser lord) as well as the equivalent in gold. On his way to Edo, he stopped at Fushimi castle to visit Torii Modotada, on whom he had conferred the custody of the castle. It was a poignant moment, for both knew that war was now inevitable, and that Lord Torii had the vital task of holding up the likely enemy advance on Ieyasu's forces. Both knew it was the last time they would meet. Hurrying on, for time was now of the essence, Ieyasu carried on overland to his own territory in the Kantō region, centred on the small town of Edo. He arrived there on 10th August.

According to Adams' account, the *Liefde* was still at sea after three weeks of stop-start sailing. Passing by the tip of the Miura peninsula, a name by which Adams himself was to be called in future, they turned north to enter Edo Bay. A short while later the ship rounded another headland to reach a small but well-sheltered stretch of water forming Uraga harbour, where a few ships were already moored. His first impression was that the place was quiet and somewhat isolated, being surrounded by low-lying hills. The town itself stretched along both shores of the bay, and perhaps Adams' thoughts were drawn back to the River Medway and his own hometown of Gillingham. If the comparison sat well in Adams' mind, that would have been good because, however much the crew desired to continue their voyage, this place was to be their new home. The *Liefde* had finally reached the end of its long, long journey.

****

The story of William Adams' first ten years in Japan, which ended with him being made a samurai, is told in Act Three: Captain Adams and the Shogun.

APPENDIX

Chronology of the Voyage of the *Liefde*

The following tabulation highlights all the dates offered in Adams' two letters of the voyage as well as those in de Weert's account. The dates in Adams' letters are sometimes written using the Julian calendar (J) and sometimes the Gregorian one (G). All the dates in de Weert's account are expressed according to the Gregorian calendar. De Weeert's account effectively ended on 10th September, 1599, and dates given below that in the same column are conversions from Adams' use of the Julian calendar, or corrected dates in the cases where Adams has clearly made an error (for example, the day his brother was killed).

CHRONOLOGY OF THE VOYAGE TO JAPAN

According to Adams' letter to his wife: 1605 dd.mm.yy (G or J)	According to Adams' letter to 'Friends': 1611 dd.mm.yy (G or J)	Description of the event	According to Sebald de Weert's account: 1600 dd.mm.yy (G) dd.mm.yy (G)
	23/24.07.98 (G)	● (Probably) the crew of all ships in the fleet boarded for the last time at Rotterdam	
24.06.98 (G)		● The fleet departed the roads at Rotterdam	27.06.98
		● Departure from England	15.07.98
05.07.98 (J)		● Incident off Cape St. Vincent	10.08.98
		● Shooting incident on Barbary Coast	19.08.98
		● Came to Saint. Iago, Cape Verde Islands	31.08.98
21.08.98 (J)		● Attacked fort	03.09.98
		● Stole millet from villagers on Isla de Brava	12.09.98
15.09.98 (G)		● Departed Cape Verde Islands Course SE	15.09.98
	Mid-September	● "...we came to the Line" (equator). This is certainly mistaken Admiral Mahu died during the night. Adams wrongly states this was at 3 degrees south. He may have meant 3 degrees north.	23.09.98
		● Course changed from SE to SSW and later to WSW	29.09.98
		● Course changed from WSW to ESE	06.10.98

147

148

Date	Event	Date
	Position recorded as 1 degree 40 minutes south	27.10.98
	Changed course for Isle of Annobon, from ESE to NE	02.11.98
	Arrived unexpectedly at west coast of equatorial Africa	03.11.98
	Arrived at Cape Lopez	09.11.98
12/13.11.98 (?)	Departed Annobon. This is certainly mistaken	
	Departed Cape Lopez	08.12.98
	Arrived at Isle of Annobon	16.12.98
29.12.98 (?)	Departed Coast of Guinea. Presumably Adams means the fleet left the equatorial African region	
	Departed Isle of Annobon	02.01.99
	Main mast of *Het Geloof* falls into the sea	09.01.99
	Repairs completed on *Het Geloof*	14.01.99
	8 and a half degrees south. Sighted Ascension Island in the distance	22.01.99
	42 degrees south. Man hanged for stealing bread	10.03.99
29.03.99 (G)	Land sighted	
	Land sighted again, off Port St Julian according to Adams	03.04.99
03.04.99 (G)	Came to the Strait of Magellan	06.04.99
06.04.99 (G)	Dropped anchor at Penguin Island	08.04.99
08.04.99 (G)	Weighed anchor, but delayed voyage according to Adams, and continued voyage according to De Weert	10.04.99
10.04.99 (G)	Reached Cape Froward	17.04.99
	54 degrees south. Anchored in the bay later named De Cordes Bay	18.04.99
	Captain Bockholt died	28.04.99
	Eight days taken to construct the sloop *Postillion*	16-24.07.99
	Departed De Cordes Bay	23.08.99
24.08.99 (J)	Exited the Strait of Magellan	03.09.99

	● Exited the Strait of Magellan. This is certainly mistaken	
	● De Blijde Boodschap breaks bowsprit. De Hoop sails on alone	07.09.99
	● De Liefde and De Blijde Boodschap separate from other ships	10.09.99
	● Adams mistakenly writes October for September.	19.09.99
24.09.99 (?)		
09.10.99 (J)	De Liefde and De Hoop re-unite at sea, but separate again after '8 or 10 days'	
29.10.99 (J)	● Adams mistakenly writes October for September.	08.16.99
	De Liefde reaches the Chilean coast at 46 degrees south. Anchor is weighed twenty eight days later	
01.11.99 (J)	● De Liefde comes to the Isle of Mocha. De Hoop had departed from there the day before.	11.11.99
02.11.99 (J)	● Shore-party lands at Cape Lavapié	12.11.99
	● Second landing by shore-party, and Thomas Adams is killed. In the letter to his wife Adams states this was the next day, ie. 13.11.99. On the third day, ie. 14.11.99, De Liefde sailed for Isle of St. Maria and met De Hoop there.	13.11.99
09.11.99 (?)		
27.11.99 (G)	● De Liefde and De Hoop depart Isle of St. Maria	27.11.99
22/23.02.00 (J?)	● A great storm is encountered in the north Pacific and De Hoop is seen for the last time	05.03.00 (?)
24.03.00 (J)	● The island of Una Colunna (Southern Iwo Jima) is sighted, and an accurate fix of position obtained	04.04.00
11.04.00 (J)	● Mainland Japan (probably Shikoku) is sighted	21.04.00
12.04.00 (J)	● Arrived at Bungo (Usuki)	22.04.00
19.04.00 (G)	● Adams states he sighted Japan on this day, after four months and twenty-two days since leaving Chile. It is not clear if he dropped anchor in Bungo on that day, although this is the generally accepted	

149

12.05.00 (J) date of his arrival today, in Japan

● Arrived in Osaka 02.05.00

Adams mistakenly states he arrived in Osaka on 12th May, knowing that he actually arrived on the 2nd, but meaning to write 22nd April, because his wife only understood the Julian calendar. He simply added 10 days instead of subtracting. In the same letter he clearly states he was in Bungo only 9 days before being taken to the palace at Osaka on a fast ship - a galley

REFERENCES

Barreveld, D. J. (2001); *The Dutch Discovery of Japan: The True Story Behind James Clavell's Novel SHOGUN*, Writers Club Press, San Jose.

Burney, J. (1806); *A Chronological History of the Discoveries in the South Sea or Pacific Ocean, Volume 2: From the Year 1579 to the Year 1620.* Nicol, Payne, Wilkie and Robinson, London. (Facsimile edition by Cambridge University Press, 2020).

Cooper, M. (ed.) (2001); João *Rodrigeus's Account of Sixteenth Century Japan*, The Hakluyt Society, London.

Corr, W. (1995); *Adams the Pilot: The Life and Times of Captain William Adams 1564-1620.* Japan Library, Curzon Press, Richmond, UK.

Dainihonshiryō (1901~); 343 vols. The Historiographical Research Institute of Tokyo University, Tokyo.

Egerton, H. E. in Ward A. W. and Leathes S. M. (eds.) (1934); *The Cambridge Modern History; Volume 4, The Thirty Years War.* University Press, Cambridge, UK.

Farrington, A. (1991); *The English Factory in Japan, 1613-1623*; (2 vols.). British Library, London.

Fury, C. A. (2002); *Tides in the Affairs of Men: The Social History of Elizabethan Seamen, 1580-1603*. Contributions in Military Studies, Number 214; Greenwood Press, Connecticut.

Guleij, R. and Gerrit, K. (eds.) (2017); *The Dutch East India Company Book*. WBOOKS, Zwolle, Holland.

Hubbard J. (2012); *Japoniae Insulae: The Mapping of Japan. Historical Introduction and Cartobibliography of European Printed Maps of Japan to 1800.* Houten, Netherlands.

IJzerman, J. W. (1915); *Dirck Gerritsz Pomp, alias Dirck Gerritsz China. Der Eerste Nederlander die China en Japan Bezocht; 1544-1604.* Linschoten Society, The Hague.

Keuning, J. (ed.) (1940); *De Tweede Schipvaart der Nederlanders naar Ooste-Indie onder Jacob Cornelisz van Neck en Wybrant Warwijck*. Linschoten Society, The Hague.

Massarella, D. (1990); A *World Elsewhere; Europe's Encounter with Japan in the Sixteenth and Seventeenth Centuries*. Yale U. P., New Haven.

Milton, G. (2002); *Samurai William: The Adventurer Who Unlocked Japan.* Hodder and Stoughton, London.

Mori, Y. (2020); *Miura Anjin – Sono Shōgai to Jidai.* Tōkyōdō Shūppan, Tokyo.

Purchas, S. (1625); *Purchas his Pilgrimes; In Five Bookes.* Henry Fetherstone, London.

Rogers, H. T. (2016); *Anjin: The Life and Times of Samurai William Adams as Seen Through Japanese Eyes.* Renaissance Books, Folkstone, UK.

Rundall, T. (1850); *Memorials of the Empire of Japon in the XVI and XVII Centuries.* Hakluyt Society, London.

Schilder, G. (2017); *Early Dutch Maritime Cartography: The North Holland School of Cartography (c.1580 – c.1620).* Koninklijke Brill NV, Leiden.

Schütte, J. F. (1980); "Visita do Superior Jesuitico de Osaka à Casa de Will Adams (Osaka, Julho 1600)", *Centro de Estudos de Cartografia Antiga, CXXXVI (Secção Lisboa)*, 209-232.

Sugden, J. (2006); *Sir Francis Drake.* Pimlico, London.

Tanakamaru, E. (2010); *Miura Anjin 11-tsū no Tegami: The Eleven*

Letters of William Adams. Nagasaki Shinbunsha, Nagasaki.

THIUT: The Historiographical Institute of the University of Tokyo (1978-1980); *Diary Kept by the Head of the English Factory in Japan (Diary of Richard Cocks, 1615-1622)*, (3 volumes), Tokyo.

Wieder, F. C. (ed.) (1923-1925); *De Reis van Mahu en De Cordes Door Straat van Magalhaes Naar Zuid-Amerika en Japan, 1598-1600;* (3 volumes). Linschoten Society, The Hague.

Wilson, D. (2003); *A Brief History of the Circumnavigators: The Pioneer Voyagers Who Set Off Around the Globe.* Constable and Robinson, London.

NOTES AND SOURCES

The story of the Mahu Expedition and the voyage of William Adams and the *Liefde* to Japan is contained in two primary sources. The first of these are two letters Adams wrote – to his wife Mary, in 1605, and to 'Unknown Friends and Countrymen' in Bantam (Java), in 1611. Both tell the story of the voyage, of the arrival of the *Liefde* in Japan, and of Adams' interrogation by Tokugawa Ieyasu in Osaka castle. They are generally consistent, one with the other, except in the dates Adams records for various events. This is because in the first letter Adams usually writes dates according to the Julian calendar (which his wife would also have used), and in the second letter he invariably refers to the Gregorian calendar.

Various transcripts of these letters exist, including in Purchas (1625), Rundall (1850), Farrington (1991) and, more recently, Tanakamaru (2010). Apart from the latter, which was deliberately written using modern English syntax and spelling, there are small differences between the other versions due to mistakes made when contemporary copies were made from the original letters. Purchas is preferred here because, in part, he claims to have made his transcripts from the original versions, though these are now lost. The other reason is that Purchas can be readily accessed on the internet, using *archive.org*. The particular copy of the book which I have used, and which has been made available for worldwide public consultation is from the Sir Francis Drake collection held at the Library of Congress. All pages cited in Act Two belong to this volume.

The other main primary source for this story is commonly known as 'the journal of Captain de Weert's voyage in the *Het Geloof*' or, by its proper name *Wijdtloopich Verhael* (The Long Story). As explained in the text, it was originally published by Zacharias Heyns, a friend of the erstwhile captain of the *Het Geloof* shortly after the return of that ship to Rotterdam in July, 1600. Although in large part based on a journal kept by the barber-surgeon on the voyage – Barent Jansz Potgieter – the account also drew on various observations made by various surviving crewmembers of the ship, including Sebald de Weert. In Act Two it is referred to throughout as 'de Weert's account'. It is recounted, in full, in F. C. Wieder's three-volume *"De Reis van Mahu en de Cordes Door de Straat van Magalhâes Naar Zuid-Amerika en Japan"*, published by the Linschoten Society of Holland, 1923-1925. Volume One contains information pertinent to the voyage itself, including useful lists of the ships and crewmen involved, as well as de Weert's account. Volume Two concerns the Magellan Strait and the chart of the Strait drawn by the navigator on the *Het Geloof* (Fig. 5). Volume Three is mostly devoted to the activities of the *Liefde* survivors after 1600, but also includes Purchas' transcripts of the letters William Adams wrote to his wife and to 'Unknown Friends', in English. There is also a brief chapter covering the possibility that Adams' crossing of the Pacific Ocean took him close to the Hawaiian Islands.

Wieder is an invaluable source and fortunately belongs to a set of publications by the Linschoten Society which have been digitized and made freely available on-line at *Werken Uitgegeven Door De Linschoten-Vereeniging*. The same series includes a volume by J. W. IJzerman (1915) on the topic of Dirck Gerritsz Pomp, one of Adams' crewmates, who surrendered to the Spanish in Chile, in 1599. This work contains some rare Spanish commentary on the events at the Isle of Santa Maria in that year, which sheds important light on the circumstances in which Adams and his fellows escaped from Spanish attempts to capture the *Hoop* and the *Liefde* there.

Apart from these Spanish and English transcripts of original source materials, almost all the content of Linschoten Society output is in Dutch. Drs Dirk Jan Barreveld's book on "The Dutch Discovery of Japan" is almost entirely derived from Wieder, and can be taken, for the most part, as an English translation. Caution must be applied, however, because the extracts have been chosen selectively and it is not always clear exactly what parts of Wieder have been quoted in translation. It is, nevertheless, the best introduction to Wieder for those without knowledge of the Dutch language.

Another invaluable primary source which has only come to light in recent years are the actual charts which Adams carried aboard the *Liefde*. Although monochrome photographic reproductions of them were published by the Linschoten Society in 1940 (Keuning, 1940; Charts VI-VIII in Appendix LXXI), the location of the original charts in the Tokyo National Museum went relatively un-noticed until recently. Now, colour reproductions from the digital archive of the museum have made them more accessible and they can be viewed on-line. Knowledge of Japanese will help in any search, but with perseverance both the Indian Ocean and Atlantic Ocean charts can be found under the title 'Seiyoujizu' with Accession No. A-9350, and with Image No's. C0012130 and C0012131 respectively. The 'Cornelius Doedsz' chart can be accessed using that name, and Acc. No. A-9412, Image No. C0010694.

A final primary source material used towards the end of Act Two is the Dainihonshiryō: an enormous collection of documents relevant to each year of recorded Japanese history. Most volumes (out of a total of 343) offer printed transcriptions of surviving official (including *bakufu*) papers at national and provincial levels. Here, for example, it has been used to trace daily movements of Tokugawa Ieyasu when William Adams was in Osaka, though no transcription of his interrogation exists. Dainihonshiryō (meaning 'big collection of Japanese historical source materials') has been compiled by The Historiographical Institute of the University of Tokyo since 1901, and the project continues today. All volumes are available on-line, but navigation is very complex and knowledge of Japanese language is essential.

This source is relied upon heavily for all subsequent Acts in the story of William Adams and will be referred to in more detail in subsequent 'Notes and Sources'.

ENDNOTES

[1] Adams wrote two descriptions of his voyage to Japan, one in each of the first two letters he sent home; in 1605, to his wife, and in 1611, to "Unknown friends and Countrymen". This extract is taken from his second letter, as recorded by Purchas (1625; Vol. 3, 125).

[2] John Davis was born around 1550 in Devon and was one of the most colourful and enterprising of Elizabethan sea-dogs. From 1585 to 1587 he led three expeditions to discover the North-West Passage in the general area of Greenland and Newfoundland, reaching the latitude of $72°_N$ before being turned back by the Arctic ice-pack. He captained the small 20-ton sloop *Black Dog* during the armada campaign, then joined Cavendish's ill-fated Second Expedition in 1591. During this voyage Davis attempted to sail through the Magellan Strait to discover the North-West Passage from the 'far-side' of America, but bad weather prevented him doing so. On the return voyage he was the first Englishman to 'discover' the Falkland Islands. He was employed on various expeditions by Sir Walter Raleigh in the mid-1590s before joining the Dutch voyage to the Spice Islands in 1598. He sailed with Sir James Lancaster on the first English East India Company expedition to the Far East 1601-1603, returning with a handsome personal fortune. He was murdered near modern-day Singapore by *wako* ('Japanese') pirates in December, 1605, whist sailing on his third voyage to the region with the 'interloper' Sir Edward Michelborne.

[3] Many of the names of countries, territories, and towns in this region have been changed in recent years – often in deference to local names

used in original, or native languages. Indonesia is officially referred to as The Republic of Indonesia; the island of Java may also be called Sunda, and the township of Bantam is today referred to as Banten (near the city of Jakarta). In this account, the older, more familiar versions of names will be used.

[4] These ship names are often described by their English translations, viz: *Hope (De Hoop)*; *Charity (De Liefde)*; *The Faith (Het Geloof)*; *Fidelity (De Trouw)*; and *Glad Tidings*, or *Gospel*, or, in looser form, *Merry Messenger (Blijde Boodschap)*. The latter is also sometimes referred to by its former name: *Flying Hart (De Vliegend Hart)*.

[5] This chart is shown in Fig.5.

[6] See Act One: His Early Years, p. 99.

[7] It is not known how or why Stracey obtained a Spanish version of his name. Possibly, he had learnt his trade as navigator sailing on Spanish ships.

[8] See Figure 4a.

[9] Two other occasions when Adams was delayed on voyages while waiting for a favourable wind to take him westwards through the English Channel are recounted in Act One: His Early Years.

[10] Provinces under the control of the Spanish king in the south and west of the Dutch territories (notably Brabant, Zeeland, Holland, and Linburg – collectively known as the Spanish Netherlands) switched from the Julian to Gregorian calendars during December and January, 1582/3, a few months after the Papal edict. The other (Protestant) Dutch provinces did not officially change until 1700/1.

[11] Years later, in 1616, Adams obviously relished holding a dinner party for his English acquaintances in Japan on the otherwise obscure date of 15th December, making the point that he was celebrating

Christmas ten days *before* the festival would occur in the Julian calendar (THIUT, 1978; Vol. 1, 368). This event was described in the daily journal kept by Richard Cocks, the chief English factor in Hirado in Japan, who continued to observe the 'old-style', even to the extent that the 'New Year' (1617) did not begin until the following April.

[12] Jacob Quaeckernaeck had become captain of the *Liefde*, with William Adams aboard, by the time that ship reached Japan in 1600.

[13] Excerpt from Adams' letter to his wife (Purchas, 1625; Vol. 3, 129).

[14] In theory, the fleet had departed the Spanish Netherlands, which belonged to the Spanish crown, and so vessels from Spain, Portugal, and France (an ally) should have been considered friendly rather than enemy. This was an argument the Dutch relied upon at least twice during the expedition when themselves confronted by Spanish or Portuguese authorities. But in reality, the Dutch considered that they were in open rebellion against the Spanish, so Spanish, Portuguese and French ships were indeed considered be enemies.

[15] In the context of this kind of voyage of exploration the term 'general' was usually used as an alternative title for the admiral and should have been used in referrence to Jacques Mahu.

[16] The Dutch attacked Las Palmas on Gran Canaria at the end of June, 1599. Initially successful in capturing the city, they were defeated by a well-organized local militia when they moved inland. They set fire to the city before departing the island soon after.

[17] From Adam's letter to "Friends and Fellow Countrymen" (Purchas, 1625; Bk.3, 125).

[18] The first quote is from Adams' letter to 'Unknown Friends' written in 1611 and the second is from his letter to his wife written in 1605

(Purchas, 1625; Bk. 3, 125 and 129).

[19] Adams' accounts of their time at sea in this equatorial region are confused. De Weert's account, however, is inexplicably silent for three weeks after 6th October.

[20] Manicongo was the Portuguese term for the Kingdom of Congo, which stretched from modern-day Gabon to Angola.

[21] This quote is taken from Purchas' own summary of de Weert's account.

[22] Even sailors who were severely ill with scurvy recovered quickly after eating fresh fruit and vegetables.

[23] From Purchas' summary of de Weert's account (Purchas, 1625; Bk. 2, 79).

[24] Another, relatively unknown, English expedition led by Sir Richard Hawkins (son of Sir John Hawkins) had passed through the Magellan Strait in February, 1594. His account of the voyage was not published until 1622, but contains an interesting description of the manner in which penguins were prepared after slaughter: "First we split them, and then washed them well in sea water, then salted them: having lain some six hours in salt, we put them in a press eight hours, and the blood being soaked out, we salted them again in our other casks, as is the custom to salt beef; after this manner they continued good some two months, and served us instead of beef" (Burney, 1806; Vol.2, 125). Hawkins took 39 days to get through the Strait. After some initial successes against the Spanish on the Chilean and Peruvian coasts he was captured and held at Lima, then later at Panama, until 1596, when he was transferred to Spain as a prisoner. He eventually returned to England in 1602. Adams would not have been aware of his fate, therefore, but the crew of the *Liefde* would surely have cured

the penguins of Penguin Island in the same way that Hawkins had done.

[25] The surviving Spaniard, named Tomé Hernandez, later escaped from the English near Valparaiso in Chile, and told his story to the Spanish authorities there. A few days later a watering party sent out by Cavendish was attacked by a Spanish military force and those not killed were taken prisoner. These men were summarily executed as pirates in retaliation, it is thought, for Cavendish's abandonment of the Spanish settlers. Memories of this incident almost certainly remained in Spanish thoughts when the Dutch expedition, now led by de Cordes, arrived in Chile a few months later.

[26] This pinnace, of 15-16 tons, was the one referred to in Adams' second letter. Usually, these pinnaces, or ship's boats, were single-masted 'sloops', but the small vessel shown exiting the Strait in Hondius' chart was clearly a two-masted 'brig'.

[27] From Adams' second letter to "Unknown Friends" (Purchas, 1625; Bk.3, 125).

[28] It is possibly this date that Adams was trying to recall in his second letter when he incorrectly records that their time in the Strait ended on 24th September, albeit he was out by a month. This was not the only time Adams mistakenly recorded the date by an entire month. In fact, the date on which he thought he wrote his second letter - 22nd October, 1611 - was really the 22nd September, 1611. Probable reasons for these mistakes are explored in Act 4.

[29] The *Trouw* and *Het Geloof* had managed to stay together during fierce storms, but on 26th September they found that they were in danger of being wrecked on the mainland coast. When the storm abated shortly after, the captains decided to re-enter the Magellan

Strait to seek a safe anchorage. During October, bad weather disrupted their attempts to leave the Strait again to seek the rendezvous point, and both ships lost anchors whilst trying to maintain position against fierce winds. *Het Geloof* was nearly wrecked when more hawsers and anchor cables snapped, and the surviving crew begged Captain de Weert to steer a homeward course. Mutiny was averted, however, and both ships remained near the western entrance of the Strait until 11th December when they lost contact and went separate ways.

The *Het Geloof* lost two more anchors and, with only one left, the painful decision was taken to return home to Rotterdam. Before leaving the Strait, however, the crew encountered fellow Dutchman Admiral Olivier van Noort's ship *Mauritius*, sailing in the opposite direction. Van Noort offered as much support as he could, having enjoyed a relatively trouble-free, albeit long, voyage to this point. His expedition went on to become the first Dutch venture to circumnavigate the globe, while de Weert exited the Straight in January and made the voyage back to Rotterdam in July, 1600.

The *Trouw*, meanwhile, did escape the western end of the Strait and made it to the Chilean coast just north of the Archipelago de Los Chonos at about 41°s. Arriving 3rd March, 1600, they had already been given up for lost by Simon de Cordes. In somewhat bizarre circumstances, the ship and crew became embroiled in the native uprising against the Spanish, which had begun the previous November. Eventually leaving Chile at the end of May, fully replenished with stores, the *Trouw* succeeded in crossing the Pacific and reaching the Island of Tidore (one of the Spice Islands) on 3rd January, 1601. Two days later, 18 of the 24 crew who had survived so far were treacherously murdered by a group of Portuguese who were on the island. Among those killed were a few Chilean native people who had earlier joined the ship, and the ship's captain Balthasar de Cordes. Six survivors of the massacre eventually made it back to the Netherlands.

The full story of the *Trouw* and *Het Geloof*, after they became separated from the rest of the Mahu fleet, is recounted in Barreveld (2001), Chapters 7, 9, and 10.

[30] Two other ships of the fleet had made it to this section of the Chilean coast at this time, the *Hoop* and the *Blijd Boodschap*, and they could not have been too far away. It is possible that the *Hoop*, with the admiral aboard, had made it to the Gulf of Penas and stopped there, as was his initial intention.

[31] From Adams' letter to his wife (Purchas, 1625; Bk.3, 130-131)

[32] Captain Gerritsz and eighteen crew were taken ashore by the Spanish and interrogated, some of the transcripts of which have survived. The crew were split up and held in separate places, but all were eventually returned to Rotterdam, the last arriving there in 1605. The full story of the *Blijde Boodschap* after it became separated from the rest of the fleet is told in Barreveld (2001, Chapter 8).

[33] A fact later confirmed by Portuguese Jesuits in Japan.

[34] More than 3,000 Spanish were killed in this struggle for liberation, and 500 females taken captive. It was a humiliating defeat for the Spanish.

[35] From Adams' letter to his wife (Purchas, 1625; Bk.3, 131).

[36] The Molyneaux globes carried by Adams are described in 'Act One: His Early Years', pp. 94-96.

[37] According to Wieder (1925; 147-149), an article by Bishop Restarick in the Honolulu Advertiser, published 24th Dec., 1922, postulated that Adams was referring to the Hawaiian Islands rather than the Marianas when recounting the escape of eight seamen in the pinnace. He based this assertion on the fact that Hawaii lies directly north-west of the Isle of Mocha (on the route to Japan?); that other islands would have been encountered by Adams before reaching the Marianas; and that even though Hawaii is located at $19°_N$ inaccuracy of latitudinal measurement in 1599 meant Adams' observations could not be relied upon. Moreover, he reported that according to the Rev'd. William Ellis, who came to Hawaii in 1822 and who collected oral histories told by the native population, seven non-native men had arrived by boat on the islands long before the time of Captain Cook and had been assimilated into the local population. Recent authors on the life of William Adams such as Corr (1995; 34-36) and Milton (2002; 88) have accepted this version of events, but it is roundly rejected by Mori (2020; 137-142).

[38] This episode is recounted in 'Act Three: Captain Adams and the Shogun'.

[39] This could, perhaps, be taken to mean the date when they finally stepped ashore, which would be consistent with his other account.

[40] The *daimyō* in question was Ōtomo Sōrin (1530-1587) one of the most powerful lords in Kyushu in his day.

[41] The 26 martyrs of Nagasaki were mostly Japanese individuals who had been converted by Franciscan missionaries, but also included four Spanish, one Portuguese, and one Mexican Franciscan brothers, as well as three Japanese Jesuit converts.

[42] It was, in fact, the Japanese authorities who would determine how

anyone landing in Japan from a foreign ship would be treated. In general, the Japanese were open to prospects of new foreign trade but were wary of proselytizing missionaries who threatened colonization of Japan by foreign nations.

[43] From Adams' letter to 'Friends' (Purchas, 1625; Bk.3, 126).

[44] Japanese nouns do not have a plural form.

[45] The word '*wako*' translates literally as Japanese pirates and, indeed, many of the pirates operating in East Asian waters were of Japanese origin. The reality, however, is that *wako* were made up of people of many different nationalities.

[46] This appears to have been an instance where Adams added rather than subtracted ten days while converting from the Gregorian to Julian calendars.

[47] The word '*hatamoto*' means literally 'under the flag or banner' and is used to denote a direct retainer or appointed vassal of a Japanese feudal lord.

[48] Taken from Adams' letter to his wife (Purchas, 1625; Bk.3, 131).

[49] Adams' corrections to the depiction of Japan in the top right-hand corner of the 'Indian Ocean chart' can be seen in Fig. 2.

Printed in Great Britain
by Amazon